CONTENTS

Introduction

This short book aims to review developments in record-keeping in language and literacy. Quite apart from the impetus given to such developments by the National Curriculum, record-keeping has been an area of very rapid growth in recent years. This growth reflects an explosion of knowledge about language and literacy, and an increased sensitivity to what it is important to observe in children's use of language. Later in the book we look at some of the ideas that have changed our views about what we need to take note of in children's behaviour as language learners and language users.

This trend towards improved records of a more descriptive and qualitative kind, rather than records which merely record performance against a brief checklist, or according to standardised tests, has paradoxically coincided with pressure for more detailed numerical information for national accountability purposes. But these two developments – both the National Curriculum assessment system and observation-based records – also have a great deal in common. Both represent ways of evaluating children's progress which aim to make a wider range of behaviours *count* than the kinds of behaviour that counted in traditional assessment. This is because most traditional tests do not enable us to take account of some of the aspects of achievement that we now believe to be important. As the Bullock Report put it in 1975, 'reading ability has outstripped the available tests'. In this situation, new forms of measurement and recording are needed to ensure that what we think matters is made to count.

Though they have very different starting-points, the new developments in record-keeping and National Curriculum assessment need not be seen as being in conflict. It is apparent that the introduction of the National Curriculum has greatly stimulated work on record-keeping, even though some of the first responses to its demands have been overly schematic. Record-keeping is the essential basis for assessment, and it is now clear that qualitative, observation-based records have proved their worth in this context. Teachers using descriptive records during the first round of assessment found that they provided more than enough information to serve National Curriculum assessment purposes. As two teachers who team-teach top infants commented on their first experience of SATs:

Our first task was to tackle the teacher assessments; these had to be completed by March 31st, 1991. Fortunately, because we had our *Primary Learning Records* to refer to, this was not as difficult as we thought it would be; a lot of the evidence required was already recorded in our observations and samples.
(Sara Haynes and Sarah Howes, 'Recollections of SATs,' *Language Matters*; 2, 1991–92)

This comment makes the point that records in language have now helped to shape records in other aspects of the curriculum. Although the frameworks for record-keeping described in this book are mainly based on the observation of children's work in language and literacy, such frameworks have much wider applicability, as the recent development of the *Primary Learning Record* at the Centre for Language in Primary Education has shown. Record-keeping in language has progressed so rapidly that it has provided a paradigm for record-keeping across the curriculum. Whatever the curricular context, observation or 'kid-watching' is fundamental to assessment, and all record-keeping raises the same kinds of issues about what it is important to observe. Very often, a consideration of children's learning in language and literacy leads to a more general discussion of how children learn.

In any such discussion, we are now much more aware that we need to include information about how children learn in more informal contexts, and about their learning at home. Many records now include space for conversations with parents. If such conversations are conducted well, they can both help to forward relationships between homes and schools, and provide valuable information which teachers need if they are to build on children's existing competences.

Parents appreciate the opportunity to share what they know about their children with their children's teachers, and it is also clear that, for them, the move towards fuller records is a major step forward. These kinds of qualitative records give them an all-round picture of their children as learners. A descriptive record is easier to understand than a bare list of Statements of Attainment that have been achieved. Though parents may well continue to feel that they want information about their children's achievement in terms of the Levels of Attainment – this is inevitable in a system which has invested numerical information with so much political importance – they often see that a good descriptive record tells them more about their children's progress than a number can. More importantly still, such a record should also show how they and the school could work to support that progress.

For children, records can provide a way of reflecting on their own progress and understanding the significance of classroom activities that are not always seen as 'work' (when teachers keep records of talk in the classroom, children can begin to see that their contributions to class and group discussions are as important as their written work). Record-keeping often helps to make more explicit to children the criteria that teachers are using to evaluate their learning. It can also provide an important opportunity for self-assessment, and as children get older we may expect them to play an increasingly important role in keeping their own records.

Record-keeping, then, has something to offer all of the partners in the educational process – parents, children and teachers – and good record-keeping systems, to which all contribute, can help to strengthen this partnership. Many teachers and parents increasingly feel that this kind of informal assessment, based on teachers' records is all that is needed for National Curriculum assessment in the primary school. They call for the extension to England and Wales of the system now in place in Scotland, where teacher assessment, supplemented by informal classroom tests, is the main way of evaluating children's progress and where school results need not be published.

As we shall argue in this book, observation-based records can be more detailed and provide more important information about children's progress in languages and literacy than national tests or numerical tables of results. Informal assessment rests on description, not measurement, on the careful and structured use of teachers' observations and their judgements. Implementing this kind of assessment has proved to be a key experience in many teachers' professional development. Whatever the eventual outcome of discussions on the future of assessment in the National Curriculum, the progress that has been made in record-keeping in recent years is likely to continue to inform practice in schools and educational thinking.

TA + SATS results
= current system

CHAPTER I

Record-keeping

It's not good enough, really, to keep it all in your head . . . I know that I certainly don't remember everything that goes on, unless it's written down. I can come back to it after quite a long time when notes are written down, and it brings it all back . . .

You have other teachers like support teachers working in your classroom and with your children. *You* may have it all stored in your head, but how are they going to have access to it? You could spend a lot of time talking over each child and the stage they're at, but that's just impossible. So you have to have on-going records that are accessible to everybody . . . It's important that it is recorded so that anyone coming in and taking over from you knows where the children are, and can take them on.

In the past, school records have sometimes been regarded as a chore by teachers. They were written up in retrospect at the end of the term, or the end of the year, and then consigned to the files, or the next teacher's cupboard. It was often suspected that nobody ever consulted them.

Many teachers felt, and some still feel, that there was no need to write anything down about 'their children' – they knew them. The kind of detailed and circumstantial knowledge that a teacher gathers about a child from seeing them every day is, it is true, impossible to write down in its entirety. So teachers came to believe that this kind of informal knowledge was too difficult to record, it had to be kept 'in your head'.

But keeping knowledge of this kind in your head makes it difficult to examine your impressions of a child and reflect on them. Memory is selective; teachers may remember some aspects of a child's behaviour and fail to note others. Often teachers who have begun to keep observational records of children have been surprised by some aspects of the record, which do not tally with their previous impressions of the child's behaviour as a learner.

I started to record one child's talk, actually listening much more carefully and observing when he was working with other children. And I discovered that I had formed quite an inaccurate impression of that child's language ability. I had him down as a rather uncommunicative child, someone who had difficulties expressing himself. But when I started observing and recording I found that wasn't so at all, and it changed my view of him, and I think it made a difference to what I expected of him, and what he became able to do.

It is true that teachers have often had grounds for feeling doubtful about the value of records. Some have maintained that they preferred not to read records from the previous teacher, because these would colour their judgement of particular children, and they would rather start the year without any preconceptions. Where records have been based on nothing better than personal opinions, this attitude is understandable.

But records that are detailed and factual, and are based on evidence of achievement, are different in kind from these impressionistic records that are not backed up by any detailed observation. In recent years new forms of recording have been devised which take account of the process of learning and track this process, recording a child's knowledge, skills, understanding, interests, and responses. Teachers use a descriptive approach, keeping diaries or journals which note the contexts for a child's learning. Samples of work are kept which enable close analysis to be made of a child's current learning strategies, and which build gradually into a detailed portfolio of their achievements.

In the field of language and literacy, one major development was obviously the Primary Language Record. This Record was developed at the Centre for Language in Primary Education (then in ILEA), from 1985 to 1987 and is now in use in many schools, both in the United Kingdom and elsewhere. The Primary Language Record combined, and further developed, many of the record-keeping approaches described above. It has greatly influenced many LEA records and will be extensively referred to in this book.

> The old records could be filled in very well or really badly. Crass statements like 'She's a dear little girl' used to appear sometimes. But these new records are fact: not a teacher's opinion but a detailed picture of what the child can do.

Teachers adopting these new methods of working have discovered that these ways of recording have had significant consequences for their own professional development. An example of this is the way in which sampling and analysis of work challenges teachers to make explicit the principles on which they evaluate children's progress, and to share their views with their colleagues.

Once records are written down and are out in the open, they can become the basis for reflection, comparison, discussion between teachers, and regular review. A child's progress is made visible, not only to the teacher, but also to other interested parties, including the child, who is obviously aware of the records that are being kept, and may be contributing to them (for example, by keeping a record of books that she or he has read). One of the major advantages of good records is the way in which they can help teachers to take a closer look at what is going on in their classrooms, and improve it.

> I made detailed notes on my sample sheet for a few children and really thought it was going to be a waste of time going through the whole process again a couple of months later. But when I actually did it I was amazed at the way my thinking had changed over that time without me realising it. Now I'm really sold on the idea.

Records based on observation and on evidence can be enormously helpful to a child's next teacher because they define areas of strength and of achievement, indicate the contexts which have proved supportive of the child's learning, and note areas of need and effective ways in which the child has been helped. For instance, a child may be reluctant to write in the classroom writing area, but may readily write in the home corner, if writing is one of the activities on offer there – the next teacher needs to know this. With a clear picture of the conditions that have helped the child to make progress, the receiving teacher can plan in a much more informed way.

Where support teachers are also working with a child – bilingual support teachers or reading teachers, for example – records serve as a permanent means of communication as well as a record. Both class teacher and support teacher contribute to the record and both can see if their observations agree or if there are any marked discrepancies to be discussed or investigated.

As primary schools have become more open institutions, with a greater emphasis on whole-school policies and on continuity between classes and teachers, it has become harder to justify closing the classroom door and maintaining differing systems in different classrooms. There is a much greater sharing of practice in primary schools now, and the importance of common approaches to teaching and learning is generally accepted. Good descriptive records can provide an important way of sharing practice, sharing knowledge of children, and maintaining continuity throughout the school.

Last year I had reception children so I got the records from the nursery teacher. And the difference that it made was that I knew from Day One where the child was and how to take them on from there. In terms of their reading and their writing I had a really good picture of that child straight away and I was ready to teach them.

Last year we had one class that ended up with five different teachers (two of them were job sharing). The Primary Language Records were the only thing that was consistent for those children. We made sure that they were kept up to date so that the new teacher coming in wasn't going to waste weeks and weeks finding out in detail what the children could do.

I've got a child who has obvious special needs in that he's not writing very well or talking very well at all and he's clearly a child whom we would put forward for statementing, involving the educational psychologist. So the records have been kept very carefully and are up-to-date and detailed. When the educational psychologist comes in we're able to say – this is how this child has been doing in language. Then the educational psychologist hasn't got to start from scratch gathering information from the teacher.

Schools have found that, though record-keeping may initially seem a chore, it can actually support their practice and come to seem much less problematic. It may even make life easier by providing a clear structure for observation. The need to observe children in the classroom has been helpful in more general ways, often making it necessary for teachers to look in some detail at issues of classroom management and develop practice in this area. Teachers have pooled their solutions to the practical question of how to manage observation, and this has sometimes affected other aspects of the school's organisation. Good record-keeping across classes and year groups both requires and promotes team work.

Where a school wants to focus on a particular area of the curriculum, or a particular issue, record-keeping can help. If everyone on the staff agrees to keep detailed records with a definite focus, these records can be used as a basis for discussion in staff meetings, can provide factual information, and can help the staff to see how policy in this area can be developed.

Special needs is in our development plan this year. We want to use the language records as a way of consolidating our policy and directing special needs thinking – it should provide us with a framework.

One of the reasons why record-keeping has assumed so much importance in recent years is that it offers a sound alternative to more conventional ways of assessing progress. Developments in record-keeping have reflected strongly felt needs for forms of assessment that are compatible with current practice in the field of language and literacy.

In reading, for instance, more holistic methods of teaching mean that teachers are emphasising other aspects of reading progress than simply the ability to decode print to sound. The old ways of gathering information (standardised reading tests, checking progress through a graded reading scheme) do not match the practice in many classrooms, and do not provide sufficiently detailed information to help teachers identify children's needs. This leads to a need for measures of reading that will take into account a broader range of competences. Through record-keeping, measures of reading have been developed which reflect practice more closely, and enable teachers to record the full range of their observations.

Detailed record-keeping enables teachers to note when a child's reading or writing behaviour changes significantly. One of the most significant moments in reading development, for instance, comes when a child begins to pay more attention to print, to slow down, and to correct their own reading. Record-keeping can help to highlight moments like this.

> There was a girl in my class who seemed to be making no progress at all, and I was getting worried about her, because it was towards the end of the first term in the top infant year. And then one day she decided to make a book which was really a retelling of a book she knew well, it was The Gingerbread Man. She dictated the story to me, we made a book of it, and she read it to me and to anyone else she could find. I would notice her carrying this book around all day. And by the end of the term she could read, her whole attitude had changed, and she knew she could do it.

Another reason why schools and teachers need an alternative to conventional methods of assessment in language and literacy is because assessment always influences teaching and affects people's ideas about what counts as achievement. Reading tests that focus on simple word recognition or on decoding can have a backwash effect on practice and may lead to an overemphasis on some aspects of reading. Alternatives to these tests must therefore be found if they are not to dictate the educational agenda. Increasingly, in many systems, teachers and other educationalists have turned to record-keeping as an alternative to the traditional tests.

Record-keeping has now been given special prominence by the National Curriculum system of assessment. The Educational Reform Act, with its statutory requirements for recording and reporting, has put record-keeping high on the agenda for curriculum development in schools and local education authorities. The National Curriculum imposes new demands on schools and teachers to record children's knowledge, skills and understanding in all areas of their work in ways that will support assessment and forward planning and provide a basis for reports to parents and for moderation at Key Stages.

From the early days of the National Curriculum, in the TGAT Report and through many official publications relating to the National Curriculum, there has been a constant emphasis on teachers' records as the source of the information that teachers will need in order to assess children in terms of the National Curriculum Levels of Attainment.

This has created wholly new functions for teachers' records. As well as serving a formative purpose, providing information for teachers about a child's pattern of learning and development, they are now expected to be the basis of summative assessment in the National Curriculum. This function also implies new audiences for teachers' records – audiences such as other teachers, and LEA moderators – as records become part of the evidence to be shared in the moderation process. The introduction of a new range of functions and audiences puts a good deal of pressure on teachers' records, and makes them potentially more *public* documents than they have been up till now. This change in the status of records can be illustrated by reference to the Primary Language Record.

When the Primary Language Record was developed, the range of its functions was well defined, and was to a certain extent mirrored in the two-part structure of the record. Figure 1 on p. 15 shows the kinds of functions that the Primary Language Record was expected to fulfil, which ranged from the classroom-based function of providing detailed information about a child's language and literacy development, to the more public function of improving communications between home and school on a child's progress. Similarly, the range of audiences included – at one end of a continuum from personal to public – the teacher herself, and, at the other end, LEA audiences, such as educational psychologists and inspectors. The Primary Language

Record Observations and Samples met the needs of the teacher herself and her immediate colleagues, while the main Record was a more public document with a wider potential audience.

From Figure 2 (p. 16) we can see that the range of both functions and audiences has increased significantly as a result of the introduction of the National Curriculum. Now that records are expected to be the basis of assessment in the National Curriculum it is harder to divide the more personal and teaching-related functions for records from their more public functions. Whereas teachers' own records would not, in the past, have been handed on from teacher to teacher, they may now need to be kept and passed on as evidence of children's achievement. These considerations give record-keeping a higher status than it has had in the past, but they also spotlight teachers' informal records in an unprecendented way.

Despite this increased emphasis on teachers' records, there has been remarkably little in the way of practical guidance about approaches to record-keeping or examples of possible formats to follow in official documents about the National Curriculum. Because record-keeping is both part of the on-going business of teaching, and also the basis for assessment in the new system, it has tended to fall down a gap between the National Curriculum Council and the Schools Examination and Assessment Council. This is unfortunate because it is probably the area where both primary and secondary teachers have been most in need of help and guidance in the early stages of the introduction of the National Curriculum. Moreover, uncertainty about the details of

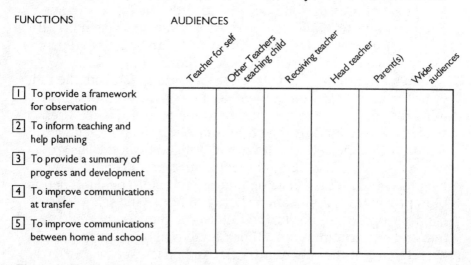

Figure 1 The Primary Language Record *functions and audiences*

FUNCTIONS   AUDIENCES

	Teacher for self	Other Teachers teaching child	Receiving teacher	Other Teachers in school	Head teacher	Parent(s)	LEA moderators	Wider audiences
1 To provide frameworks for observation	X	X						
2 To inform teaching and help planning	X	X	X					
3 To record progress in the National Curriculum	X	X	X					
4 To be the basis of Teacher Assessment	X	X	X		X			
5 To provide evidence for moderation	X	X		X	X		X	
6 To provide a summary of progress and development	X	X	X		X	X		X
7 To improve communications at transfer			X		X			X
8 To provide a framework for reporting to parents on:								
a children's achievements in the National Curriculum						X		
b children's progress and development in a broad context.						X		

Figure 2 Records within the National Curriculum *functions and audiences*

the new assessment system has made it even harder for schools to work out their own forms of record-keeping.

The only detailed guidance which was issued to schools on the subject of record-keeping was the three-part SEAC Guide to Teacher Assessment which was distributed in 1989. This was essentially a SATs training manual in disguise. The model that it put forward for the curriculum and for teaching was completely assessment-led: the pack proposed that teachers should spend their time setting up activities mainly for the purpose of assessing them. Teaching and learning were thus reduced to a series of 'TAT's (Teacher Assessment Tasks). This pack realised some of the worst fears about the influence of assessment on the new system, and it met with a very critical response from schools and LEAs. The only record-keeping formats it included were tightly geared to National Curriculum assessment; in some cases they were merely checklists of the Statements of Attainment. Since that time SEAC has also issued a report on Primary Records of Achievement, but this publication contains no detailed examples of record-keeping.

The initial panic reaction in some schools to the statutory requirement for record-keeping has been to focus solely on the Attainment Targets, and produce a whole series of tick sheets to record children's progress on the ever-proliferating criteria of the National Curriculum. This response was undoubtedly fuelled by the SEAC Teacher Assessment pack, with its proposals for a continuous classroom programme of testing children against individual Statements of Attainment. The Secretary of State was reportedly unnerved when met in schools by teachers waving sheafs of grids and checklists – the inevitable consequence of such an approach.

It is not surprising that the initial flight into 'tick sheets' is being challenged as both unworkable and ineffective by researchers such as Stephen Hopkins, who explains:

> Many schools have already devised record sheets that allow each of the 200 or so Statements applicable to Key Stage One, for example, to be recorded for each child several times . . . It is now clear that the task of assessment as currently conceptualised by these schools is totally unmanageable and professionally misdirected. There would seem to be little point in accumulating vast, detailed and analytical records of the child's performance if it is unclear what consequent actions are appropriate.
> (from a paper prepared for the BGC/BBC Managing Assessment Conference, 1990)

There clearly remains a need, however, for comprehensive, continuous recording systems to support National Curriculum assessment and to lend it credibility and substance. It seems obvious that such records will need to be narrative or descriptive in character if they are to reflect teachers' observations accurately. The DES booklet *From Policy to Practice* spoke of the importance of the 'rounded qualitative judgements' that narrative records provide. Columns of ticks and numbers cannot reveal anything in detail about a child's learning. Checklists have proved to be an unhelpful way of recording because they only direct attention to a narrow range of behaviour and therefore pre-empt the teacher's judgement of what is noteworthy in the child's language and literacy learning.

Even the best checklist, which identified and focused on aspects of learning which were universally acknowledged to be of prime significance, could not possibly contain a complete list of all the elements that it might prove important to note about a particular child's progress. To discover what a child is able to do, the teacher needs to attend to their individual behaviour as a language user over time and in different contexts, and to become aware of how that particular child goes about their learning, as well as seeing what their learning has in common with that of other children. The knowledge gained in this way will naturally feed straight back into a teacher's planning and teaching.

Grids and checklists will not, either, be of much value as evidence of children's attainments in the National Curriculum. They offer only the barest kind of record, and provide no real contextualisation of the minimal information they contain. Teachers engaging in group moderation, or discussing their assessments with visiting moderators, will need more substantial evidence of what children can do to enable them to compare their judgements, and agree interpretations. A row of ticks is very superficial evidence of the complex learning involved in, for example, becoming a writer.

Though language and literacy records will serve as the basis for assessment in the National Curriculum, this does not mean that they need to be tightly geared to the Attainment Targets. The National Curriculum in English is in any case far wider than the content of the Statements of Attainment, which are boiled down to a bare minimum from the rich curriculum set out in the Programmes of Study. Records need to reflect children's experiences of this broader curriculum. As long as they are generally compatible with the National Curriculum and record progress in the areas of Talking and Listening, Reading and Writing, they should – together with other evidence, such as a portfolio of writing – contain enough information for assessment purposes.

Even though it should prove possible for teachers of English to keep records that are mainly narrative or descriptive in character without the back-up checklists that will be necessary in some other subjects with more Attainnment Targets and Statements of Attainment, they may still find it helpful to review their records periodically, perhaps once a term, with particular reference to the Statements of Attainment to ensure that they will have sufficient evidence to arrive at appropriate judgements in terms of National Curriculum towards the end of the Key Stages.

In 1990 the Secretary of State for Education, then John McGregor, said that: '. . . there can be no question of requiring teachers to keep detailed records of their pupils' attainments against every single one of over 200 statements of attainment.'

However, it is becoming clear that the demands of record-keeping in the National Curriculum could lead in either of two directions. It could give rise to poorer practice in this area, reviving discredited and minimal models such as checklists, and making it more likely that children will be regularly assessed in terms of a crude grading system. Or it could stimulate the development of narrative and descriptive records which will serve as the basis of assessment, but which will also go beyond this assessment function to provide a detailed profile of a learner's strengths and needs. The latter kind of record is a true 'formative' record. In order to understand more fully the role of teachers' records in relation to the National Curriculum we really need to consider the difference between formative and summative assessment.

═══ *Formative and summative assessment* ═══

The term 'assessment' covers a variety of practices which serve different purposes. The two major kinds of assessment with which we shall be concerned are formative and summative assessment. *Formative* assessment is assessment which is part of the daily business of teacher and learning, and it is inseparable from observation. Through observation teachers gather information about children's learning which helps them in their teaching and their planning. This kind of constant feedback is formative assessment. Formative assessment is not the same as continuous assesment; it does not imply that children are being graded daily. It is just the process of evaluating what children are doing in a very informal way so as to be able to teach them better. The obvious vehicle for this kind of on-going formative assessment is a teacher's record.

Summative assessment, on the other hand, is, as its name implies, a summarising of all previous observations and evaluations, a summing up of all that is known about a child's learning. Summative assessments are often expressed as numerical or letter grades, as in GCSE grades. Summative assessment draws a line under all of a child's previous performance, and provides a judgement on it.

The TGAT Report, which provided the blueprint for the National Curriculum, originally recommended that the new national assessment system should be 'essentially formative'. Only at school-leaving age ought there to be a need for a final summative assessment. The Report recognised that assessment can get out of hand if it is given too much importance in a system, and stressed that it should be 'servant not the master of the curriculum'.

Yet at the same time, the TGAT Working party suggested that it ought to be possible to combine formative and summative purposes through the ten-level ladder of attainment that it was recommending as the basis of assessment at the Key Stages. A child's progress up this ladder could give both feedback to the teacher about the child's needs as a learner, *and* provide a numerical grade which could be shared with parents and wider audiences. TGAT also thought that these grades could be used for the purposes of *evaluative* assessment (the assessment of the system itself), as they could be aggregated and made to yield statistical information about the performance of children in the system. This information would be published, and would provide a constant check on standards of education, something that politicians have been wanting to measure for some time.

The problem about the TGAT's recommendations was that they tried to combine functions that assessment experts have always advised should be kept separate. Formative assessment cannot be combined with summative assessment without summative assessment coming to dominate the partnership. The kind of crude grading that the ten Levels of Attainment represent may, unless we are careful, come to outweigh all the other more qualitative information that we have about children. We have yet to see the full effects of this kind of regular grading of children every two or three years or, if a system of annual reporting to parents in terms of these National Curriculum levels is introduced, every year. Past experience of such assessment practices suggests, however, that the effects could be serious.

Concerns such as these have sometimes been made light of by government spokesmen who argue, for example, that the overwhelming majority of seven-year-old children will be assessed at the same level, Level Two. This may be true at age seven, but it will certainly not be true at the subsequent Key Stages. The full implications of this model, and what it is likely to do to the organisation of schools (how will eleven year olds who are functioning at Level Five in History share a curriculum with those who are still working at Level Two?), have yet to be felt.

As far as teachers are concerned, formative assessment will go on being the main kind of assessment that matters for teaching and learning. This is because it is the only kind that feeds directly back into their teaching. A grade or a test score provides no information about the detail of a child's performance, and is therefore not helpful in identifying their needs. Effective teaching needs fuller and more diagnostic or descriptive information.

The Statements of Attainment are all about achieved behaviours, things that the child can already do. Teachers need to know more than this in order to help children make progress. They need to know more about a child's behaviour as a learner, and about what the child can do with support, or in collaborative situations, as well as when they are functioning in isolation. Some children can achieve a great deal in particular contexts, and teachers need to be aware of these areas of strength so as to know where to direct their help and their teaching. Teachers will be interested not only in the products of a child's learning – the finished pieces of work – but in the process of that learning. By observing how a child goes about a particular task they will be able to find out more about the child as a learner than will appear from an examination of a finished product, which may reveal nothing about their understanding.

It is also very important to consider, in any record, how a child feels about learning, how involved they are in their reading or their writing, and how confident they appear. Teachers know that this affective aspect of learning can make all the difference to a child's development because it really provides the impetus for all they do. They need to be just as concerned and involved with this side of learning as with the content of a child's learning, their 'knowledge, skills, and understanding.'

It is important that we should not let the summative gradings of the National Curriculum, and the 'minimal competency' statements which make up the Attainment Targets, dominate formative assessment and record-keeping. The best way to ensure that they do not is to keep formative and summative assessment distinct and separate in our model of the assessment process, and in our record-keeping systems. Figure 3 (p. 22), a diagram of the teaching, learning, and assessment cycle, offers a way of thinking about formative and summative assessment which separates out these two functions.

In Figure 3 we can see the continuous cycle of planning, teaching and learning, observation and record-keeping, and further planning (informed by records) which goes on in the classroom every day. Formative assessment is firmly part of this cycle in the shape of teachers' records. But summative

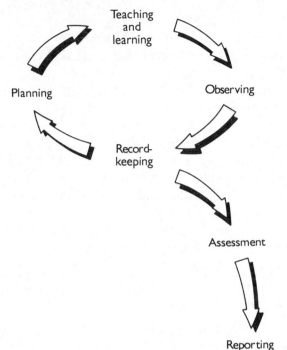

Figure 3 The planning, teaching and learning, observing and recording cycle

assessment, in terms of the National Curriculum Levels of Attainment, is an offshoot of the cycle because it does not happen daily or weekly but at the Key Stages or – in some schools – annually. These summative assessments are then, as the diagram shows, reported to parents and wider audiences.

Summative assessment is based on teachers' records, which are also their way of recording formative assessment. This means that such records will have to contain enough information to enable teachers to arrive at a summative judgement in terms of the National Curriculum Levels of Attainment. As we have already indicated, in English this will not be too difficult because there are relatively fewer criteria to attend to, and most of them will be part of what a teacher thinks it important to focus on in children's language and literacy learning.

In order to provide a basis for summative assessment, and subsequently for moderation, teachers' records will have to provide adequate evidence of children's achievements as language users. The kind of evidence that might be included in records, and the role of evidence in National Curriculum assessment, is discussed in the following section.

Statutory assessment in the National Curriculum has concentrated teachers' attention on the need to have evidence of children's attainments. Sometimes there will be 'products' of learning in the shape of writing, drawings, plans and models, but quite often learning does not result in this kind of tangible outcome. In English, keeping evidence of children's progress in writing is relatively straightforward, but it is less easy to see what evidence of their progress in speaking and listening or in reading should be kept. In assessing these 'process' aspects of learning in English, teachers' written notes and records become crucial evidence of a child's achievement.

In their advice for Key Stage 1 assessment, the SEAC encouraged teachers to gather such evidence:

> You may also find it helpful to make very rough notes of what the child said, so that you can refer to them if you have any doubts when recording later.

> Such notes, especially if they are dated and the context noted on them, should normally provide more than adequate evidence of the child's attainment. (School Assessment Folder)

Where no 'product' exists, then, it will be down to a teacher's skill in observation and their professional judgement to interpret a child's level of understanding in a particular area, and those records will be accepted as adequate evidence of the child's learning.

While teachers are not required to report formally against individual Statements of Attainment, or to place the child in relation to Levels of Attainment at any times other than at the end of the Key Stages, they do have a statutory duty to monitor and report on a child's progress in the National Curriculum. This means that teachers will have to be aware of the Statements of Attainment as they keep their records, and in some cases they may have to extend their record-keeping procedures to ensure that evidence of achievement in a particular area of the curriculum is taken into account. For example, EN2 requires that children: 'listen and respond to stories, poems and other material read aloud, expressing opinions informed by what has been read'. Listening to stories and talking about them has been one of the longstanding pleasures of the primary classroom. Teachers have always monitored, in a general way, children's responses to stories read aloud, but from time to time they will now need to keep some informal record of children's comments.

Sometimes, even if there is a tangible outcome to the learning, there should be a note of explanation by the teacher to accompany the 'product'. A piece of writing by a young child, may not mean much to someone who knows nothing about the child or the circumstances of the writing; the teacher will probably need to record what the child meant the writing to say, and comment on what it shows about his or her progress in order to draw out its significance in the child's development.

It may therefore be helpful to include with some pieces of writing a short written note about their context. This will enable the teacher to remember more about the way the child went about the writing (e.g. if it was unaided, if it was a first or a final draft), and will provide helpful information for other teachers and visiting moderators. Many teachers now keep regular 'samples' of writing, which involve reviewing a particular piece of work in some detail with a child, and noting the exact circumstances in which it was produced. The Cox Committee recommended that these 'process' aspects of writing should be given as much attention in teachers' assessments as the final 'products'. As discussed in more detail in the next section, such records can provide vital additional information, such as the support on which the child has drawn.

What is noteworthy?

If schools are to develop a coherent assessment programme, then teachers will have to agree upon what they consider it is important to collect and to record. They will need to have some shared sense of what is noteworthy about a child's development. In *A Guide to Teacher Assessment*, it is suggested that the Statements of Attainment themselves represent all that is noteworthy and that teachers should make them the focus for the gathering of evidence:

> The noteworthy growth points in a pupils's knowledge, understanding and skill have been described in the Statements of Attainment.

One problem with focusing exclusively upon the Statements is that, even if they enjoyed the full confidence of teachers, they represent two-yearly benchmarks and are therefore less than comprehensive in charting a child's progress. What is noteworthy in terms of formative assessment will depend upon what the teacher needs to know on a day-to-day basis to support the child as a learner. M. Simpson argues against limiting assessment to the 'tightly specified course objectives' of the criterion-referenced model, because:

> Assessment must . . . extend beyond the simple determination of the extent to which they have learned as intended to the discovery of what they have *ACTUALLY* learned.

> ('Why criterion referenced assessment is unlikely to improve learning', *The Curriculum Journal*; 2, 1990).

In suggesting that the focus must be on the child rather than on a set of pre-specified criteria, this argument gets to the heart of the matter. For most of the time, as they follow the Programmes of Study in their day-to-day work with children, teachers will be gathering evidence for formative assessment based upon children's actual behaviour across a wide range of activities, including evidence of attainment of the Statements of Attainment for which, as we have noted, there must be appropriate provision. So the complex task of tracing and identifying the child's development cannot depend solely upon matching performance to pre-specified criteria, it must also depend upon the teacher's observation of the child as a learner in different situations. The child's actual, possibly unique, response to activities, and what this shows about the extent of their understanding, represents what is noteworthy in the growth of an individual child. Such rich and relevant recording carried out in the context of the Programmes of Study, and with due regard to the criteria of the Statements of Attainment, can also provide ample evidence of a child's level of achievement for statutory reporting purposes.

It is clear, then, that recognition of the complexity of children's learning and how much is likely to be 'noteworthy' is a first step in the consideration of evidence, which itself falls into two parts: the record of what a child actually did, or said, or produced, and the circumstances in which it was done. The circumstances will include a note of who initiated the work or activity, whether the child worked alone, in a group, with a particular friend or someone chosen by the teacher for a collaborative task. The support which was offered to or sought by the child, and the support the child actually acted upon are also important to record. It is often only possible to reach a fully rounded assessment of a child's writing when some of these questions are answered. This is demonstrated by the sample of writing by M:

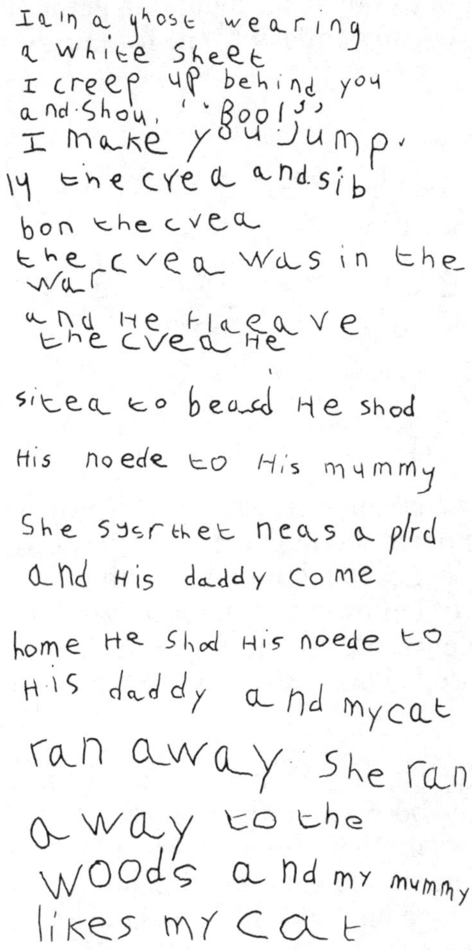

I am a ghost wearing
a white sheet
I creep up behind you
and show, "Boo!"
I make you jump.

ly the crea andsib
bon the cvea
the cvea was in the war
and He tlaeave
the cvea He

sitea to beard He shod
His noede to His mummy
She sysrthet neas a plrd
and His daddy come
home He shod His noede to
His daddy and mycat
ran away. She ran
away to the
woods and my mummy
likes my cat

Figure 4 A sample of writing by M

This example looks at the context of a piece of writing and shows how recording the context enables an assessment to be seen in its proper perspective and enhances its formative role. The writing falls into three separate parts, each written in a different context.

Part 1 M had chosen to work with a group of her peers who were very excited by story writing. All the group made books and wrote their own stories. M had consistently been encouraged to try to write independently, but had always firmly refused to do so, asking her teacher for all but the simplest spellings. On this occasion she was drawn along by the excitement of the group, and her solution was to find a book from the class library and begin to copy it out so that she could join in the fun of book-making. There was not sufficient time for her to complete the book.

I am a ghost wearing
a white sheet
I creep up behind you
and shou, "Boo!"
I make you jump.

The context in which this part was written reveals her interest in book-making and her need to be part of a group activity. It shows her lack of confidence in attempting spellings, and perhaps in creating a story of her own, and the fact that she has not sought the support of her peers, even though she chose to work with them. She has used another strategy – selecting and copying a story book.

Part 2   The following day M took up the writing once again but could not find the book from which she had been copying. She would not choose another. The teacher sat with her and suggested that she should continue to write the story for herself. No spellings were given but M was encouraged, word by word, to draw on what she knew and write for herself. She developed the story without help and seemed to know exactly what she wanted to say.

   The context in which Part 2 was written shows M's commitment to the creation of a story book and the importance she initially attached to continuing with the original story. However, within this new context she showed an ability to write independently, developing her story and attempting spellings. Her enjoyment of the teacher's undivided attention and encouragement were supporting factors which enabled her to grow in confidence, organise her thinking and demonstrate hitherto unrevealed skills.

ay the cvea andsib
bon the cvea
the cvea was in the
war
and He Flaeave
the cvea He

sitea to beacd He shod
His noede to His mummy

She sysrthet neas a plrd
and His daddy come

home He Shod His noede to
HIS daddy

the cover and slipped
down the cover
the cover was in the
way
and He fell over
the cover He
started to bleed He showed
His knee to His mummy
She says that needs a plaster
and His daddy came
home he showed his knee to
His daddy

Part 3 Finally, the teacher moved on to work with other
children, but continued to observe M from time to time. Without
the teacher's personal attention and continuous encouragement
M did not continue with the detailed story she had been creating,
and abandoned her independent attempts to spell unknown
words. She changed her writing strategy once again: this time she
drew upon a small repertoire of known spellings in order to
continue the writing. The storyline changed as it became
dominated by the spellings she knew.

and my cat
ran away she ran
away to the
woods and my mummy
likes my cat

In this third context M has been thrown back on her own resources, with clear consequences for her creative writing. The urge to create a storybook is still strong and she shows that she knows a number of correct spellings – and *knows that she knows* them.

With these contextual notes it is possible to make sense of the changes in the writing and to look at what has stimulated the child and the different kinds of support she has used or failed to use at each stage. This information will be vital for an assessmen of the piece and also for the future planning of help for M in her writing development.

The circumstances of this piece of work, and the teacher's close involvement, made its significance immediately apparent. But gathering evidence more widely has its problems. Often noteworthy developments are only clear with hindsight: one chil wrote several versions of the same story at intervals over a perio of some eight months; viewed separately they did not appear significant, but a retrospective analysis provided marvellous evidence of development in many different areas.

Where there is a product such as writing, it is useful and comparatively easy to retain a great deal of material, but teache cannot write down everything that children do and say in a day and they will need to consider how to develop systematic and manageable approaches.

Sometimes a teacher may note significant comments made by child, for example, when one child produced a remarkable piece of work and explained to her teacher exactly how it had come about, the teacher immediately wrote down the comments and kept them with the work. But observing and briefly recording a sample of *each* child's talk at a particular point in the year, or during a project or group activity, is useful and ensures that individual children do not go unnoticed by the teacher in a busy classroom.

As teachers become completely familiar with the National Curriculum it will be necessary for them to develop common understandings across a range of issues if they are to have confidence in the quality of their assessments. The criteria established by the Statements are only the starting point for a process which must gradually take account of these issues.

Evidence of attainment will be profoundly affected by the task itself. Some tasks will inevitably be more supportive, or lead to more complete evidence, than others. This difficulty has already been recognised in areas where many teachers are unused to gathering evidence, such as technology or speaking and listening, and it is not surprising that teachers have shown some interest in the non-statutory SAT's. Once removed from the compulsion and competition of the statutory SATs programme, such common tasks are useful as trial material which can be used in the classroom as starting points for discussion and may lead gradually to agreement between teachers on what could be considered as appropriate tasks. Teachers can focus on the real issues of how far such tasks represent good class practice, and how likely they are to produce evidence for valid assessments.

In evaluating a piece of evidence, a teacher will also have to decide how typical it is of the child. Is it indicative of complete mastery in a particular area? How many times, or in how many different situations must a child demonstrate knowledge? To some extent this will depend upon the kind of knowledge. Once children have acquired factual knowledge, such as the names of letters in the alphabet, they are unlikely to forget them and evidence on one occasion is probably enough. On the other hand, a child's understanding of, for example, punctuation, and their ability to punctuate a piece of work correctly, grows more slowly and is likely to vary considerably with the difficulty of the piece itself and the extent to which the child's attention was focused on punctuation at the time. Evidence will need to be gathered on a number of occasions in order for a teacher to come to a well-balanced decision on the level of a child's understanding. This problem was not created by the National Curriculum and is by no means new to teachers, but the existence of common criteria does not necessarily ensure common agreement on the kinds or quantity of evidence needed in any area. This can only be established gradually through discussion and example, as C. Connor points out:

A degree of consistency in what and how to record will only be achieved by recognising the complexity of learning and by involving teachers in the process of reflecting upon that judgement.

('National Curriculum Assessment and the primary school: reactions and illustrations of emerging practice'; *The Curriculum Journal*, 1, 1990)

Are there common interpretations of the criteria being applied? Many of the statements are capable of very different interpretation: consider for example the requirement that children: 'read a range of material with some independence, fluency, accuracy and understanding'. Decisions have to be made about the level of difficulty of this 'range of material', of what constitutes evidence of 'independence', 'fluency', 'accuracy' and 'understanding' and to what extent 'some' qualifies these requirements. The starting point for such decisions is discussions by teachers within individual schools.

The need for consistency in the National Curriculum has provided an opportunity for teachers to explore not only its new requirements but also many fundamental issues concerning assessment and the provision of adequate evidence of children's learning. It can provide a new impetus for reflection and discussion, beginning within individual schools and extending more widely between schools and across age ranges.

CHAPTER 2

Observing Language and Literacy Learning

═══ *Examples of significant observation* ═══

This chapter contains examples of teachers' records of children's progress in language and literacy. These records are based on observation and they provide rich evidence of children's learning. Most of these records are drawn from the Primary Language Record or from the work of teachers who are experienced in it; one or two come from other sources. We begin with an example which is not a teacher's record, but an example of close observation of the kind that helps us to appreciate the varied influences on children's development as readers, writers, and language users.

═══ Example 1   Researchers' observations of a ═══ six-year-old boy

The following extract comes from *Inquiry into Meaning*, an observation-based study of children learning to read made in a group of American classrooms. The researchers worked closely with the teachers involved, who kept detailed notes on the children under observation, and who were interviewed at several points during the two years for which the study continued. In addition, the researchers visited the classrooms and made their own detailed observations of the children in the study. All these observations produced very rich evidence of the children's individual learning styles, and of the factors that seemed to contribute to their progress in reading.

The observational record for each child was read and discussed by several other people involved in the research, who then identified what seemed to be the most important themes running through individual records. This extract comes from the case study of a child known as Louis and is taken from the first section of the case study, the thematic heading for which is

'Incremental manner'. One of the things that emerged most clearly from Louis' record was his step-by-step approach to most activities, and this was particularly marked in his construction activities:

Preference for materials with multiple units

Louis's partiality to materials that consist of parts and pieces comes to light early and proves lasting. During the first observation he is found building with Lego, his favourite material and almost exclusive activity during choice time for the entire two year period. His teacher describes these constructions:

> His lego constructions are quite intricate, elaborate, they have an inside to them . . . structures look like tractors, buildings, police cars. Starts new one every day – kids have a chance to put things away if they want to continue working on them – he doesn't do that. Very organised around Lego, knows what pieces he needs, fishes them out of the box (October, 1st grade).

When not building with Lego, Louis turns to blocks, to Multi-Rollaway, and occasionally to Lincoln Logs. During maths, he will use cuisenaire rods, when available, to build elaborate constructions. All these materials consist of small discrete components, having hard-edged, mostly geometric shapes that come in multiples but in a limited variety of shapes. They are found in good supply in Louis's classroom.

His affinity for objects that have parts is reflected in Louis's choice of books during quiet reading time. He begins the first year by selecting a series of books depicting heavy machinery and vehicles, such as trucks and tractors, in rich and realistic detail. He pores over these diagram-like pictures, unable to read the compact and rather technical text that accompanies them. He is also drawn to the one type of book that can be said to have parts, the pop-up and mix-and-match books with segmented pages that can be permuted and arranged in many configurations.

The inclination to segment is also revealed in the way Louis learns to read. He treats letters and words as discrete units, acquiring them one at a time. As a result, his teacher is aware of his progress in uncommon detail. At the beginning of the first year, he knows all except four lowercase letters. By October, he acquires 5 sight words. In January he is able to use initial consonants and has accumulated 23 sight words. Similarly, in his writing, letter follows letter in the early months of the school year; later, Louis proceeds to writing one word at a time, using a fair bit of erasing and reworking. (Bussis *et al.*, *Inquiry into Meaning*)

This detailed case study is based on much fuller observational records than could normally be kept by a classroom teacher with thirty or more children in the class. However, it is quoted here to show the value of keeping a broad observational record which goes beyond noting a child's involvement in activities which are obviously language or literacy related. Louis' interest in Lego and similar constructional materials is very much a part of his overall pattern of learning, and a clue to his individual style in approaching reading. The case studies in *Inquiry into Meaning* look at children as learners across the whole range of their learning, and pay particular attention to their drawing, their model-making, and their dramatic play. By so doing, they stress the interrelatedness of these different symbolising activities, and the very personal character of learning.

This brief extract gives only a flavour of the careful observation contained in these case studies, but its line of thought is provocative. Many teachers will recognise this type of learner, and appreciate the analogy that is being drawn between Louis' interest in construction activities, and his organised and incremental approach to learning to read. One of the values of a relatively open record, such as a diary of observation, is that it allows children's different aproaches to learning to be noted, and their individual learning patterns to be analysed. This is helpful to teaching because teachers can then build on children's areas of strength; their observations will inform their decisions about when and how to intervene. This record makes it very clear what kinds of books and activities most attract Louis, and would enable a teacher to plan future learning experiences for him.

Example 2   A reading diary for a boy with special education needs

The diary in Figure 5 is taken from the records of a teacher from a special school for children with mild learning difficulties. It is a simple record of all the occasions, over two terms, when she heard O read or read with him, giving brief remarks about each reading session. O entered the school in Janaury 1990.
Unlike a fuller diary of observations, such as the Primary Language Record 'Reading Diary', a list of this kind only shows how the child behaves as a reader when the teacher is present. It does not reveal much about his pattern of reading outside these occasions, how frequently he chooses to read, what kinds of texts

15.1.90 Each Peach Pear Plum (O's own choice)
I read it to him. A bit thrown by reading
a whole book to me — intensity of contact
almost too much for him. Not very confident
— _over focuses_ on grapho-phonic cues.

26.1.90 Don't Forget the Bacon
I read it to him. We tried to read it back.
Doesn't remember stories all that well. Try
on some of our own class books. _Needs time
to settle in class_.

31.1.90 The Ten Little Piglets (O's choice)
We read it together twice. O joined in
second time but it was a bit of a
struggle. Doesn't really read for meaning.
N.B. — get O to choose books he _really likes_.

7.2.90 Not Now Bernard (O's choice)
O read this with obvious pleasure and
enjoyment, commenting on text, laughing at
pictures. He decided to do his own book —
uses own invented spellings etc.

29.3.90 Mr Gumpy's Outing
Read v. well — using all cueing systems.
Focusing on words. Using phonic cues as
well — good in a sense — occasionally don't
make sense though. Is much more relaxed.

5.4.90 Bears on Wheels
Read rather slowly — made one comment, 'Look
like acrobats'. Found it quite difficult to predict.

2.5.90 In the Night Kitchen
I read it to O. He liked the book 'because
Mickey went up in the aeroplane'.

3.5.90 Angry Arthur (O's choice)
O liked the book because 'he keeped

getting angry!' O 'gets mad 'when his 'sister beats (him) up'. The book was quite difficult for him – some words difficult to predict, but he gathered confidence as he went on, using context/lang./pics for cues.

8.5.90 Hello, Goodbye
We read it together – difficult to predict – O found it difficult.

13.5.90 Dear Zoo (my choice)
O read well. Needed help to get started with 'They sent me...' but then picked it up. Made some good guesses using memory, picture, context. Self-corrected 'long' to 'tall' ie. focuses on print & individual words. Still over-dependent on visual cues.

18.5.90 Each Peach Pear Plum (O's choice)
O said he liked the book because 'it's got all people in it'. Read it well – needed help with some words. Still lacks confidence a bit when it comes to guessing/predicting.

24.5.90 Each Peach Pear Plum
O read it again – read word for word. Tends to use look of words – grapho-phonic cues – doesn't self-correct even if it sometimes doesn't make sense.

1.6.90 Dean's Week
O read well. Substituted was for went every time. We talked about it – continued to read 'was'. Needs to read lots of texts with strong rhythms/ meanings.

4.6.90 The Very Hungry Caterpillar
O read well – especially at first. Still tends to guess words with inappropriate meaning based on phonic appearance of first few letters.

Figure 5 Reading diary for a boy with special educational needs

he reads apart from books, and so on. However, it does give a good impression of a succession of his encounters with particular books, and it also records, most helpfully, the titles of the books that he chooses to read in this situation.

Some of these choices recur in what seems to be a significant way. *Each Peach Pear Plum* is the first book that O selects to read to the teacher, although in fact she reads most of it to him in the end. On this first occasion in January, the teacher is well aware that O is getting used to her and to the situation of reading through a whole book with the teacher (he may not be accustomed to being given so much attention, or even to reading a whole text in this way). Later in the school year he returns to this book twice more, and now he can read it well. It is a supportive text for someone like O, who is over-dependent on print cues, because the rhyming text and the pictures encourage prediction. O particularly likes examining the pictures – which are very much part of the game of reading *Each Peach Pear Plum* – and says he likes the book because 'it's got all people in'. The huge cast of *Each Peach Pear Plum*, which includes so many familiar nursery rhyme and fairy tale characters, is one of its attractions, and spotting the characters as they recur is part of the game.

In O's first weeks in the class, the teacher is most concerned to put him at his ease; he seems to be struggling, and she guesses this is because he needs more time to find his feet in the class. He may be trying too hard with his choice of books, and she makes a note to herself to encourage him 'to choose books he *really likes*'. Until O feels more relaxed and at home it is going to be hard for her to see what his strengths and difficulties as a reader really are. But by February, O is more relaxed, is showing more signs of enjoying what he is reading, and has begun to make comments on the books. Now it is possible to analyse his reading more closely, and the teacher begins to jot down what she notices about the way he approaches reading aloud – he finds it difficult to make predictions, and tends to focus mainly on phonic cues, sometimes to the detriment of the meaning. This continues to be the pattern of his reading until the end of the school year, though sometimes he is particularly relaxed and confident, and then he seems more able to make good guesses and use language and context cues.

The teacher also records O's reactions to the books he reads. Some books engage him more than others, and *Angry Arthur* in particular, though it is not an easy book for O, seems to be one which means something personal to him; a remark made by him about it connects it with his own life. Books like this, and like *Not Now Bernard*, which deals with powerful feelings as well as being funny, may be particularly significant for children's learning. The teacher stresses the value she sees for O in books with strong *meanings* or strong *rhythms*; she wants him to meet books where the intrinsic interest of the story or the rhythmical pleasures of the language are marked. This will help O to realise that reading is more than decoding print, and focus his attention on other elements in the text, which will be supportive to his development.

These brief entries in a diary would enable the teacher to look back over six months and consider O's progress and her own interventions. It would also give another teacher a good picture of what kind of reader O is, and what kinds of texts and support it might be important to offer him. And finally, it would provide evidence of O's achievement, for himself, for his parents, and for the purposes of assessment.

Example 3   A teacher's scrapbook of a six-year-old girl's writing

Many teachers find that a scrapbook is a good way to keep examples of children's writing together (the more formal term for this is 'portfolio assessment'). They may buy commercial scrapbooks for this purpose, or make their own out of sugar paper. Not all that a child writes need be kept in the scrapbook of course, it is simply a way of preserving examples of writing so as to be able to record development in a very concrete way. Often the child is involved in choosing which pieces of writing should be put in the scrapbook, and this creates a good opportunity for teacher and pupil to review the contents and to discuss progress together. It can be very interesting and encouraging for young writers to see how much more they are able to do towards the end of a school year than they could do at the beginning.

Examples of writing that are kept in this way need to be labelled with the date and a brief contextualising comment to ensure that they make sense when the teacher comes to look back on them or use them for assessment purposes later. As we have seen, any piece of writing is only the tangible outcome of what can be a lengthy process, and has little meaning without some indication of the circumstances surrounding the writing. In the extracts from the scrapbook shown in Figures 6–9 the teacher has not written a lengthy commentary, but her short comments go straight to the point and provide key information about the contexts for these samples of writing, including information about her own part in the process, and the extent of her intervention.

The samples span a period from October to February in this girl's middle infant year (year one of the National Curriculum). This is a period of particularly rapid development for S, and the samples reveal this clearly, and enable anyone looking back through the scrapbook to relive some of the excitement of S's growing confidence and sense of her own capabilities.

19th October

Much class discussion following the hurricane. S part of a small group writing – unwilling to write alone, so worked with me one to one and we wrote together in 'try out' book. Encouraged her to try – let own spellings stand and only came in when asked. Gave her 'along'. Read final piece through & she wanted spellings corrected – ticked all her correct efforts – she liked this. She made a fair copy.

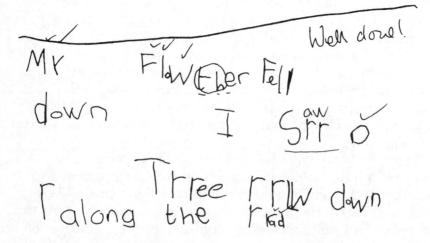

Figure 6a Scrapbook of a six-year-old girl's writing *19th October: try-out book*

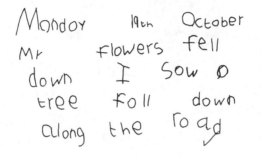

Monday 19th October
Mr flowers fell
down I sow o
tree foll down
along the road

Figure 6b Scrapbook of a six-year-old girl's writing *19th October: fair copy*

25th November
Class watched Jill Murphy story 'On the Way Home' on TV – loved it, talked about it. Told them all to write on their own. S wrote straight into exercise book (first time) – did not use 'try out' book. She did not ask for spellings to be corrected so I left them, made no comment.

Wednesday 25th November
the Goods is rfdrd
Me and I GoTrWay
and I keinG He
Ond He frLddrw

Figure 7 Scrapbook of a six-year-old girl's writing *25th November*

and the doG Bhdh
it shr and the
CAr want in to
shr house

one day the cat and the doG
Cemh oet of her was weating Fror
house and She the cat to camh
Sorh a doG and awt ovh the house
the doG camh upto and the want awt
her the bk Door

and KLMd uP and the caT
the roFh and GoTh cLh ner
She kLMd ord farSh tb kaMh
the Fasr and and the doc Was
eh Sapd FriTT ard the
doG ranh awr ✓
Louely story.

Figure 8 Scrapbook of a six-year-old girl's writing *14th December*

Wednesday 25th November
The ghost is after
me and I got away
and I kicked him
and he floated away. (Text from Figure 7, p. 40.)

14th December   (See Figure 8, p. 41.)

S part of small group writing own stories. Did not ask for help with spellings but wanted to read over each page – needed help from me and rest of group to take story forward. Think she liked the attention. Story more than twice as long as anything written so far. Completed in morning session – story typed, made into book.

February   (See Figure 9, p. 43.)

Written & illustrated in one morning at my suggestion. (S loves Avocado Baby story). No help with spellings or story.

The first sample in October shows S as a hesitant writer, unwilling to write independently, and needing maximum support from the teacher. In this piece the teacher records that she worked one-to-one with S, but it is significant to note that she did so in order to encourage S towards greater independence, and only intervened when S directly asked to be helped. S is concerned about spelling, and likes it when the teacher goes over her first attempt to show her exactly where she has got things right. Working in a 'try out' book has obviously helped S to feel she can take risks with spelling.

By November, S is prepared to write directly into an exercise book for the first time without using a 'try out' book. The occasion for this piece of writing seems from the teacher's comments to have been particularly stimulating, not only for S but for the other children as well. All of them had enjoyed seeing *On the Way Home* on the television, and of course the shape of this story positively encourages children to join in and make up their own tall stories to match those Claire invents in the book. S has had a really good idea, very much in the spirit of *On the Way Home* in which she gets the better of a ghost. Her description of what happened is vivid ('I kicked him and he floated away') and catches the boastful tone of Jill Norman's text. She is learning to make written language work and to manage both the 'encoding' element of writing, and the composing of a text for a reader.

In December, we find S writing confidently and independently. Her story is, the teacher notes, twice as long as anything she has previously done, and this indicates her

One day the
Avocado baby's
Mummy Fidd
a Avocado
Pare In the
Bol and the
Avocado baby
eat it
uP. OL
Soiing and he bekm

Figure 9 Scrapbook of a six-year-old girl's writing *February*

increasing engagement in writing, and her growing sense of herself as a writer. This is an accomplished piece of narrative; like the previous story it deals with a threatening enemy being routed – the cat manages to chase off the dog with the help of her friends. There is suspense in the story as the dog waits for the cat at the front door and then becomes more cunning and begins to hunt her down systematically, going round to the back door and climbing up to the roof. Finally cunning defeats cunning as the cat's friends appear. The triumph of the ending is signalled clearly in the text ('and the dog was FRITT').

The teacher notes that S needed the support of the group in discussing the development of the story, and this is not surprising as it is the longest written narrative that S has yet attempted. It is notable that she can now accept help from the other children in the group; she no longer needs the one-to-one support of the teacher. She is more confident about attempting spellings, and her spellings are becoming closer to conventional spellings overall. This is her first draft, of course, and the teacher notes that it was subsequently reworked and made into a book.

By February, S has become a remarkably prolific and confident writer of stories. Figure 9 is the first page of her seven page story about the Avocado Baby, based on the book that she enjoys so much. It is probably the fact that she has the framework of a known story to build on that enables S to write at such length on this occasion; given the opportunity, children often choose to retell stories that they like or use them as a starting point for their own version. The teacher notes that S is now working quite independently and is able to sustain this unsupported activity over an entire morning. S no longer needs constant reassurance or help with her writing, and one reason for this is obviously that she is now prepared to take considerable risks as a writer, and will attempt spellings of words she does not yet know well. This enables her to be much more ambitious in what she writes, though of course she will, through revising the story with her teacher, or through seeing it typed up in standard spelling, be able to compare her own good guesses at words with the adult forms.

These four texts give a remarkably full picture of S's very rapid development in writing over a period of only four months. Together with the teacher's brief comments, they make up a valuable record of this extraordinarily important period in S's growth as a writer. The major factor in this growth seems to be S's increasing readiness to write independently, and in particular to attempt the spellings of words she does not yet know without constant recourse to the teacher. This enables her to write at much greater length, and to draw on her knowledge of books and narrative to create her own complete stories, which already show her competence in managing an extended text.

Example 4   A teacher's diary of a six-year-old boy's talking and listening

The following example is drawn from Elizabeth Dawson's article on 'Sampling Talk' in the magazine *Language Matters* (1990, No. 1). Talk is not an easy aspect of language to record. An open diary format is in many ways the most flexible way of noting any examples of talk that seem significant, but the very openness of this format is sometimes problematic as it seems to offer little structure for the observation. Teachers may feel unsure about what to look for in talk, and about what counts as significant in a child's behaviour as a talker. The Primary Language Record 'Diary of Talking and Listening', which Elizabeth Dawson was using for her observations, encourages teachers to look at both the social contexts for the child's talk, and also at the learning contexts in which the observations are made. A child may behave differently in different contexts, as Philip does in the observations that follow. Elizabeth Dawson explains in her article that she tends to make most recorded observations of children whose development is slower or is less obvious to her. Philip was such a child, and she recorded eight observations of him altogether in the course of the year. Five of these eight observations are included here, together with Elizabeth Dawson's further notes on her original record.

Observation 1 (September)
Playing a 'Feely Bag' game, which involves describing objects hidden in a bag to a group. When it was Philip's turn, he described his object (a pencil): 'It's got a pointed end'. This was a description used earlier by other children. When the others asked for a further clue he could not extend the description but said 'I don't know'.

This observation supported my informal mental assessment of Philip at the time. He is quite a shy little boy, rather a loner, and his speech is sometimes very indistinct (he had some speech therapy last year). Early in the school year, his responses to my attempt to engage him were very often one-word responses, and he sometimes gave up if I had difficulty understanding him.

Observation 2 (October)
The whole class were listening to an older child explain and demonstrate how he cared for his hamster. Philip made his first voluntary contribution in the context of such a large group. He asked, 'How do you clean its cage?'

This observation notes a new development. Up to that time, Philip had often seemed not quite 'with it' when the whole class was together. He often sat on the edge of the group and appeared not to be paying very much attention to our discussion/the story etc.

Observation 5 (February)
Increasingly more forthcoming and on the ball. He really likes to volunteer personal information to me now and is quite often bringing things in to show to the whole class . . . On his birthday, he confidently told the whole school what he had received (though interestingly, in this rather daunting situation, it was a one-word utterance and rather indistinct). He argued, the following day, that 'It's still my birthday, because I'm going to have a party tonight.' He is now consciously amusing, and likes at times to play to the gallery.

This observation details signs of Philip's increasing confidence in a range of situations: with me, with the class, and with the school.

Observation 7 (March)
After some more work about the pitch of musical instruments, Philip said, 'The big one makes a little note. The little one makes a big note'.

He was making observations and drawing conclusions, although he didn't use the terms 'high' and 'low' to describe the pitch of the notes.

Observation 8 (May)
My challenge to the group was : 'Make your piece of plasticene float'. Philip rephrased this: 'You've got to think how the plasticene's going to float'. He was the first in the group to succeed. Delighted with himself, he then took on a consultative role to help the others. He told another child 'Get rid of the

holes'. And when the plasticene still sank, he explained: 'It's got no holes, but it's too heavy'.

In a group, Philip was able to gain confidence from his practical abilities, and this seemed to encourage him to talk fluently and enthusiastically.

This series of observations shows considerable development in Philip's oral language over the school year, and clearly demonstrates that his ability to use his talk for learning is closely linked with this growing social confidence. He is readier to contribute in small groups and in the context of practical activities. Later in her article, Elizabeth Dawson notes that 'The discipline of writing down *some* of my observations about a child seems to sharpen my ability to make and recall many more mental notes about him/her.' Record-keeping develops the habit of observation, and also ensures that children like Philip, who is unobtrusive in class, do not go unnoticed. Teachers who have used diaries in this way over long periods often say that, even when they think they know a child well, the 'discipline of writing down' observations often leads them to see things that they had not previously noticed at all, and which may sometimes surprise them.

Example 5   A Primary Language Record reading sample of a six-year-old girl's reading

The next example comes from the reading record for a six-year-old bilingual girl. The teacher is using the 'Reading Sample Form' from the 'Observations and Samples' section of the Primary Language Record to record this child's reading on one particular occasion. This form provides a way of structuring and standardising the observation of reading. Together with the 'Reading Diary' that also forms part of the 'Observations and Samples' sheet, it gives a good all-round picture of the child as a reader.

The 'Reading Sample Form' is used when a child is reading with and to the teacher. This is a normal context in which to assess children's reading in an informal way, and the reading sample does provide a means of informal assessment. Before doing a reading sample the teacher decides which of three means of sampling she is going to use on this occasion: a running record, a miscue analysis, or an informal observation. Each of these sampling procedures in described in the *Primary Language Record Handbook*, and each involves some form of error analysis. On this occasion, the teacher is using an informal observation, but it will be apparent that her comments are informed by a knowledge of miscue analysis.

The 'Reading Sample Form' enables examples of a child's reading to be kept over time, just as writing can be kept in a writing folder. Because of its format, it also enables a child's reading on one occasion to be compared with later occasions, and in this way it should make it possible to keep track of progress in some detail. It provides a framework within which detailed qualitative information about a child's reading can be recorded.

This sample shows a six-year-old girl reading a known text, *Just Like Daddy*, which is a favourite book of hers. It used to be thought that assessing reading meant presenting children with an unknown text to read, thus making instant decoding the major focus of assessment. In the same way, reading programmes in schools put all the emphasis on reading a succession of unfamiliar texts, and much less emphasis on the rereading and revisiting of familiar books. However, it is now clear that we can learn a great deal from observing children reading texts they have already met, and that this is a good context for seeing how they operate as readers in normal circumstances, as young readers consolidate their skill mainly by practising with familair material.

Before reading *Just Like Daddy* R had read an Urdu text to the teacher; this fact may be reflected in the sample, and particularly in the teacher's conclusions about how R's reading could be further supported.

The teacher notes that R knows the book well, and that she enjoyed the reading. R reads the text with zest and expression, showing by her intonation that she appreciates its shades of meaning, and that she has understood the irony of the ending. Reading a known text enables R to bring out these finer points of the reading, because she is not entirely focused on decoding to sound.

At the same time, in the second section of the sample, the teacher is able to go into some detail about what the reading has shown her about R's ability to draw on a range of cueing systems to read the text on the page. It is clear that she is focusing upon each word and not simply remembering the text, so that her

3 **Reading Samples** (reading in English and/or other community languages)

to include reading aloud and reading silently

(Handbook pages 45-49)

Dates			
Title or book/text (fiction or information)	Just like Daddy		
Known/unknown text	known text		
Sampling procedure used: informal assessment/running record/miscue analysis	informal observation		
Overall impression of the child's reading: • confidence and degree of independence • involvement in the book/text • the way in which the child read the text aloud	R read this with obvious understanding and delight. Expressive and highly involved with this favourite book		
Strategies the child used when reading aloud: • drawing on previous experience to make sense of the book/text • playing at reading • using book language • reading the pictures • focusing on print (directionality, 1:1 correspondence, recognition of certain words) • using semantic/syntactic/ grapho-phonic cues • predicting • self-correcting • using several strategies or over-dependent on one	R knows the book well + was able to draw on this knowledge. One to one well established. Has built up a core of sight vocab. Making intelligent subst. "I washed my teeth" (face) context unchanged she did not correct. Knew the word for worm but in Urdu only.		
Child's response to the book/text: • personal response • critical response (understanding, evaluating, appreciating wider meanings)	v. involved in text. discussed pictures freely and observed many details. "Just like Mummy's" was read with relish. R. obviously aware of the irony & went on to explain that Daddy has the 'smallest fish'.		
What this sample shows about the child's development as a reader. **Experiences/support needed to further development.**	It is good to see R. reading so confidently in both Urdu + English. We should continue to encourage this - R reading aloud to the class/assembly in Urdu.		

* *Early indicators that the child is moving into reading*

Figure 10 Primary Language Record: reading sample of a six-year-old girl's reading

sense of one-to-one correspondence is 'well established'. She makes some substitutions in the course of the reading ('I washed my teeth' instead of 'I washed my face'), but these are of the kind that experienced readers who are reading for meaning often make; in miscue analysis they are known as 'positive miscues'.

Perhaps the place in the sample where R's well-established strategy of reading for meaning becomes clearest is where, realising that she does not know the English word for worm, she offers the Urdu word instead. This is really a remarkable moment in the sample. It shows that R is reading the text at a deep level of linguistic processing, she is using all her linguistic resources to make sense of it. It also shows that R feels free to draw on her knowledge of Urdu in school. She is confident that her teacher will regard this as relevant information. It seems likely that R's sense that she can use her knowledge of her first language in this way was strengthened, on this occasion, by having had the opportunity to read to the teacher in Urdu before reading to her in English. Even though the teacher speaks no Urdu, by showing an interest in R's first language she has encouraged her to make use of it here.

The sample concludes with a section which encourages teachers to reflect on what it has shown about the child' development as a reader, and how to help the child progress. In this case, the teacher notes that reading in Urdu as well as in English has been a positive experience for R, and that she should have more opportunities in school to develop her literacy in her first language.

═══ *Models of language learning* ═══

The previous section gave examples of what might be called 'significant observations' from records of children's learning in language and literacy. In these observations it is clear that the teacher/observer is focusing on details of behaviour and performance which offer good clues to the course of a child's development. The observations also note what seem to be key experiences that contribute to the child's progress. What kind of theory are these observations based on? This section gives a very rapid tour of the theoretical understandings that help us to observe children's learning in language and literacy.

Acquiring language and acquiring literacy: significant parallels
We now know that children go through a series of transitions in

their development towards adult systems of reading and writing. They gain control of adult systems with time, support, and teaching. Our picture of how this happens is heavily influenced by studies of young children's oral language acquisition, though it is clear that there are also major differences between learning language and learning to read and write – learning the written language is a much more conscious process than learning to talk. There is, however, much to learn from this parallel, and Don Holdaway and others have done a great deal to make the links between language acquisition and literacy acquisition explicit.

Learning a second language has many similiarities with learning a first language, and we no longer imagine that knowing one language 'interferes' with the process of learning a second. All of a child's experience of language learning supports their further learning in language or in literacy, and careful observation can show children drawing on their existing resources as they learn.

Psycholinguistics and error analysis
Psycholinguistics has helped us to observe reading development, and provided us with a 'window on the reading process' in the shape of miscue analysis. What we have learned from psycholinguists, like Kenneth Goodman, in this area can also be applied to writing; error analysis and the observation of children's self-monitoring and correcting strategies can help us look analytically at a child's development as a writer. Miscue analysis has helped us to re-evaluate error – it is clear that not all errors are negative, some reveal a growing understanding of the system. Frank Smith has pointed out that simplified texts can get in the way of understanding (and therefore of reading) because learners are hampered if they have to work with incomplete or incorrect information. He has also stressed the value of feedback (rather than correction) to the learner.

Stage theories of development
We have learnt a great deal from developmental psychology about what happens as children develop in language and literacy, and all our ideas about development have been heavily influenced by the work of Jean Piaget. Some researchers and writers about literacy have begun to identify 'stages' in reading or writing development that can be labelled and observed. Some of the work that has been done on writing development, for example by Temple, Nathan and Burris in their book *The Beginnings of Writing*, has helped us to see patterns of

development, and to note important steps that children are making in their independent writing, such as moving from writing 'strings of letters' towards writing in groups of letters, with the first letter representing the initial sound of a word. (Stage theories of development often tend to focus on a single aspect of development, such as encoding, rather than the whole complex activity.)

But we also know that 'stage theories' derive from a view of development that can focus too exclusively on the 'solo child', and present mental development as if it were a process of organic growth, like the growth of plants. Literacy theories that lean too heavily on traditional developmental psychology can limit our view by suggesting that all children have to go through the same invariable set of stages in their progress towards the adult system. This is, observably, not true, and there are good reasons why it should not be true. Mental development is a cultural, rather than a biological process, and it involves learning; it is a *social* process.

Vygotsky's theory of development

The other major psychologist whose work has now begun to influence the way we look at literacy is Vygotsky, a Russian psychologist whose main interest was language development. Vygotskyan psychology stresses the social nature of development and thus prompts us to give more weight to the observation of what children are doing in *supported* situations and in *collaboration* with others, not only to what they can do without help. This implies that we should be observing children learning language in a range of social contexts. A more interactional view of learning also serves to put special emphasis on the importance of teachers' interventions; we observe children in order to be better able to support their learning. This shared learning is then gradually internalised by the child.

Learners are all different

As well as being aware of the things children have in common as learners, we need to be aware of their individual patterns of learning. Careful and well documented observation, like that reported in *Inquiry into Meaning* (see pp. 33–34) is beginning to tell us a great deal about the different routes that children take to learning, and the differences in the way they use language and approach literacy. Some children are prepared to take more risks, others seem more conscious of error, and prefer not to hazard a guess until they are fairly sure that they are right.

—52—

Children's records can help to highlight their personal approaches to learning and enable teachers to plan more effectively for them.

Literacy and gender
There are other differences that affect the way that children learn. In language and literacy we have become particularly conscious of the differences between the achievements of girls and boys. At the primary school stage there is a paradox: boys generally receive more attention than girls, yet they do less well at reading and writing. In order to explain these differences, writers like Julia Hodgeon have had to consider the social meaning of literacy and explore how women and men, and boys and girls, see reading and writing. We also need to look at the kind of literacy on offer to children in the primary school and see whether there is a tendency, for instance, for the books chosen to reflect the preferences of girl (and female teachers) more closely than those of boys.

Home and school
In general we are now much more aware, through the work of Gordon Wells and others, of the fact that children's language and literacy learning begins at home and remains rooted in the home. Schools are beginning to establish closer links with homes, and to be more aware of what can be gained from talking to parents about their children's literacy experiences at home. Links of this kind can help us to avoid stereotyping children's home backgrounds. Teachers who have established this kind of dialogue with parents, by using records such as the Primary Language Record, have begun to appreciate how much reading and writing actually happens at home, and have learnt more about, for instance, the positive influence that television can exert on children's developing literacy.

Biliteracy
Such home-school links can also facilitate a sharing of information about bilingual children's progress in their first language, and the extent of their literacy in the other languages they know. This enables teachers to appreciate children's achievements more fully, and to build on them in the classroom, by encouraging children to use their first language at school, and by organising opportunities for them to read and write in their first language.

Cultural contexts for literacy

Homes provide different cultural contexts for developing language and literacy. We are now more aware, through the work of sociolinguists, and of ethnographers like Brice Heath and others, that literacy learning is culturally based. If we have more information about the nature of the literacies that children are learning, and the styles of interaction they are used to, this can have important implications for the classroom. In the past, white middle-class educationalists tended to use their own cultural standards as absolute standards, and catalogue the things that working class children and black children could *not* do. This deficit model, used in relation to children from certain groups, did not focus on their positive achievements but only on their deficiencies against a particular yardstick, and this made it impossible to build on the children's actual strengths. The need to make closer links with homes and with the different communities and cultural groups that children come from, so that home experiences can truly be the foundation for school literacy, is now much clearer, but practice still lags behind theory in this area.

Learning how to mean

Finally, awareness of difference leads us back to Halliday's perceptions about the need for learners to find their own purposes in literacy. In *Language as Social Semiotic* he posed an important question:

> What is learning to read and write? Fundamentally it is an extension of the functional potential of language. Those children who don't learn to read and write, by and large, are those to whom it doesn't make sense . . . [it] does not match up with their own expectation of what language is for.

Language and literacy growth needs to be rooted in children's sense of the meaningfulness of these processes, and in their sense that they can use them to express personal and cultural meanings.

As well as understanding the functions of literacy, it is likely that the successful learner is going to find pleasure in being a reader and a writer. We need to remember the evidence to the Bullock Committee which spoke of the experience of adult illiterates who 'had never understood from the process of learning to read that it was something other people did for pleasure.' Observation needs to look for children using literacy in purposeful, meaningful and pleasurable ways, for example, at their self-initiated activities, and at the role of these activities in their growth as language learners.

═══ *Models of record-keeping* ═══

Finally, in this section, we look at the kinds of record-keeping practices, and formats, that will facilitate the sort of significant observations that were described in the first part of the chapter and reflect the views of language and literacy development outlined in the previous section.

It may be helpful first of all to outline some of the principles that need to underlie the best practice in this area. What do good observation-based records have in common? This list attempts to define their characteristics:

- **Regular, frequent, and systematic recording**
  Observation of children goes on every day, and record-keeping needs to be part of observation. It is easier if record-keeping is systematic, so that none of the children get left out. (One of the benefits of record-keeping is that it helps teachers to see that they are giving more equal attention to children.) There are all kinds of ways of ensuring that record-keeping is done regularly and kept up to date. Teachers can keep a note in their register of the occasions when they have had a reading conference with a child, or observed their talk. A matrix such as the one in the Primary Language Record 'Talking and Listening Diary' enables this kind of information to be seen at a glance. When record-keeping is systematically organised in this way, it becomes part of the routine of teaching and is able to give a much better picture of a child's progress over time.

- **The recording of normal behaviour in favourable contexts**
  One of the major advantages of record-keeping is that it enables teachers to assess children's progress in normal classroom situations, and not in special assessment contexts. This also enables teachers to keep a record of what children can do in favourable contexts, when their interest is thoroughly engaged – children's apparent ability can vary enormously in different contexts. Recording a child's best work in this way helps both the teacher and the child, whose confidence in learning may be strengthened by knowing that their achievements are valued.

- **An emphasis on positive recording**
  The kind of record-keeping that focuses on a child's strengths, and on signs of positive developments, is likely to be supportive of those developments. When a teacher has spent time analysing what a child can do, she is in a better position to support the child's attempts. (Records that only focus on what children cannot do are almost useless; they do not offer anything to build upon.) Focusing on strengths also fosters a positive attitude towards children as learners, and this is important, as children are fundamentally affected by teachers' views of their ability. Positive recording is not bland, it is a question of describing the extent of a child's achievements as accurately as possible.

  Positive record-keeping is also important from the point of view of equal opportunities. All too often in the past, children's differences from the majority culture have been viewed as deficits, and their positive achievements (such as the ability to speak a language other than English, or a dialect other than standard) have not been taken into account. It can be helpful for teachers to consider what strengths a child has as a learner that may not have been included in their record.

- **Recording that includes evidence from home**
  Children may be very different people at home and at school, and we are becoming much more conscious now of the need to record their achievements outside school. Partly this is because we are now more aware that a great deal of learning goes on before school, and outside school, which needs to be taken into account in the classroom. Partly this move results from a much more general realisation that parents and teachers need to work together for children, and a growing emphasis on making links between homes and schools. Such links are supportive of children's learning, and particularly of the learning of children whose home languages and cultures are different from the prevailing culture of the school. Records can include evidence from home in the form of discussions with parents, or records of home/school reading schemes.

- **Records which stress the links between different aspects of language**
  Progress in one aspect of language learning is often linked to progress in another. For instance, a child's development as a

reader is obviously closely related to their writing development. Records that enable teachers to compare these linked aspects of development, and that encourage such comparisons, provide a better picture of a child's overall progress. Records that enable teachers to include information about a bilingual child's progress in their first language as well as in English also underline the links between these aspects of language development.

- **Records which view errors as information**
  Miscue analysis has encouraged us to see errors as information, and to analyse errors so that we appreciate the understandings that they reveal. (Analysis of a child's miscues in reading a particular passage may show that most of the errors are 'positive', and that they do not interfere with their overall reading of the passage.) This way of looking at errors is clarifying. Instead of being faced with a mass of 'mistakes' to be corrected, teachers are made aware of what strategies a child is using in learning language, and are put in a better position to give helpful feedback. In time, with further experience and support, children begin to correct themselves and to monitor their own errors more systematically, and teachers can encourage and model this process in conferences and shared reading sessions with the children.

- **Records which include contributions from children**
  Records that include a measure of self-assessment are very helpful to learners. They encourage children to take more responsibility for their own work, to reflect on their learning, to evaluate their progress, and to become better at monitoring what they do. Children usually appreciate the opportunity to contribute to their own records, and may also take on some of the work of organising and keeping their records up to date, selecting pieces of work to include in their folders, date-stamping their work, and so on.

- **Helpful structures for recording**
  In the past, record-keeping tended to be dominated by checklists and grids. Structures of this kind pre-empted judgement, and made it difficult to include in a child's record any observations which fell outside a predetermined set of behaviours. Teachers have been moving away from grids and checklists in their observational records, but sometimes it is difficult to know what to include in a very open record.

Structures can help by focusing attention on particular aspects of language and literacy, and by encouraging systematic observation. The best kinds of structures, however, will always be 'open structures', which allow teachers to note behaviour that they think is significant, but within a framework. The reading and writing samples from the Primary Language Record are good examples of 'open structures'.

- **Recording in different contexts and in different formats**
  A teacher cannot record all that she thinks is noteworthy about a child's progress in one type of record. For instance, some reading records will enable her to record a child reading to her on specific occasions, while others will provide a general observational record of the child as a reader in the classroom. It is the combination of these different types of recording that is powerful, and that enables teachers to compare children's behaviour in one context with their behaviour in another.

Evidence	ATI Speaking and Listening	AT2 Reading	AT3–5 Writing

Details	- Date
	- Names of talkers/listeners
	- Purposes
		- Date
		- Names and roles of readers
		  and those with whom
		  reading is shared
		- Purposes
			- Date
			- Names and roles of writers
			  and audiences
			- Purposes

Teachers'
observations
	- Observations of a) groups
	  of children, b) individuals
	- Notes on more public talk
	  occasions (eg drama
	  performance)
	- Records of discussion with
	  child
	- Records of discussion with
	  parents
		- Observations of children's
		  reading
		- Lists of books read
		- Records of discussions
		  about reading with child
		  and parents
			- Observations of children's
			  writing, with comments on
			  approaches to writing
			- Lists of writing undertaken
			- Records of discussion with
			  child
			- Records of discussions with
			  parents

Samples	- Transcripts (brief
	  extracts of talk)
	- Audio/video tape
	- Child's written response
		- Analysis of a piece of
		  reading (eg miscue
		  analysis)
		- Tape of child reading
		- Child's written response/
		  reflection
			- First and final
			  actual pieces of
			  writing, or an extract
			- Commentary accompanied
			  by folder of writing

Evidence
gathered by
children
	- Notes/preparation for
	  presentations
	- Tapes made (eg of
	  stories, radio programmes
	  with other children)
		- Lists of books read, with
		  comments
		- Reading journals
			- Lists of writing
			- Writing folder
			  with comments
			- Personal checklist of
			  points to work on

Figure 11 Making the gathering of evidence possible *English Non-Statutory Guidance*

These are the kinds of principles that mark the most developed forms of record-keeping, such as the Primary Language Record. The formats provided in the Primary Language Record give a range of ways of keeping track of children's learning, and records like this help teachers to develop their own judgements, and to become more effective observers in the classroom.

One very useful list of the forms that teachers' records can take is provided in the *English Non-Statutory Guidance*. In section E, 'Gathering Evidence of Achievements', there is a table that shows the range of ways in which teachers can record children's language and literacy progress. This is a comprehensive summary of the records that schools might choose to keep in this area of the curriculum, and might provide a framework for discussions by teachers on the subject. It also demonstrates that recording in the National Curriculum *does* need to go beyond checklists of the Statements of Attainment if it is to provide convincing evidence for assessment and do full justice to children's achievements.

CHAPTER 3

Developing Good Record-Keeping: A Whole-School Approach

══ Practical issues ══

As teachers develop their approach to recording they will need to address the practical problems of classroom management and consider how a system of record-keeping which is both feasible and effective can be organised to support assessment. Teachers will need to set aside time for observation and recording when curriculum planning. Curriculum planning itself is becoming increasingly complex as more subject teaching is specified within the National Curriculum. Most schools are based on a teacher–pupil ratio of about one to thirty, and this means that teachers will need to develop strategies for gathering and recording information which utilise all possible forms of help, and organise this within a single coherent system through the school. In most schools this will need to be viewed as a long term development in which all staff will be involved, sharing effective classroom strategies and working together to address issues which require whole-school planning. (A dynamic example of such teamwork is described in the following section, 'Conditions for the development of good record-keeping', pp. 67–72.) The practical aspects of planning will concern the management of teacher time and the organisation of records and work samples so that they are relevant and accessible.

══ Spreading the load ══

One of the new aspects of record-keeping pioneered by the Primary Language Record was the notion that a whole variety of people could contribute to records. Part-time teachers, support staff and ancillary workers often work with individuals or small groups and are in a good position to make factual notes of comments made by children or observed behaviour. They can be asked to ensure that work is dated and any appropriate contextual information provided. Parents are also gradually becoming involved. In many schools they already contribute 'home to school' information and comment on their children's reading behaviour through PACT schemes. Some of the schools who are currently developing primary records of achievement send home the notes on teacher/child reviews so that parents can read them and respond, if they wish to do so.

The responsibility for formative assessment and planning for the child remains with the teacher, but if school policy encourages the collection of a wide variety of information from different sources, then this provides a broader perspective on children's development while helping with the practical problem of teacher time in gathering that information.

===== Involving the child =====

Children themselves are potentially the teacher's greatest resource in terms of recording progress. Their participation is important not only for the practical help it can provide, but also for the way it encourages reflection and increases their involvement in their own progress.

Teachers are therefore beginning to encourage children to play an increasingly important part in the recording process. Many pupils already record the titles of books they have read, with occasional book reviews which provide evidence of their response as well as the range of their reading. In some classes children contribute to checklists of curriculum coverage by personally recording work which has been completed. Most children date their work as a matter of course, and this is being extended in appropriate circumstances to include a brief reference to context: How did the work arise? Was it their personal choice or directed by the teacher? How long did it take? Did they work alone or in a group? Occasionally, teachers ask children involved in group work to note carefully their own contribution, in some cases supported by special 'prompt' sheets.

The encouragement of self-assessment by children has been a significant development in many classrooms, and, together with review and target setting, it is an important feature of records of achievement. Self-assessment both supports the child's personal development and helps the management of recording by allowing children to make a contribution to their own records. However, it makes demands upon children to become increasingly reflective and analytical, and these are complex processes which need to be carefully nurtured as part of a wider support for children's personal development.

Teachers can begin to develop the youngest children's ability to reflect by asking them to consider the things they enjoy doing or dislike, to share their ideas with the class and to record them in different ways. Writing, drawing, tape recording can all be used.

It is also important to develop in children a concept of 'achievement' itself. Teachers can heighten children's awareness of what they are able to do by encouraging them to share with class and friends their achievements in a wide variety of areas both in and outside school. Achievement should not be viewed in a narrow sense as the mastery of some new skill, but should include the recognition of personal qualities, such as perseverance, and social development through, for example, taking responsibility. For some children, simply taking part in a particular event will be a significant achievement. Teachers can help by drawing attention to any evidence of progress and abilities, valuing them and ensuring that children are provided with opportunities to record their achievements and to share them with others.

Self-assessment involves an ability to recognise personal needs, but children will only feel able to acknowledge their needs in a classroom which has a positive ethos. Children need to feel safe from ridicule and destructive criticism. Teachers can help to develop trust within the community of the classroom by, for example, encouraging children to focus on the talents and achievements of their peers. Sometimes they may record and display these positive comments in 'walls of friendship'. The trust between children which this generates helps individuals to acknowledge their needs and promotes self-esteem.

Gradually, children may become more confident and used to recognising what they are able to do. They may need help to become reflective and to identify their strengths and weaknesses. Sharing ideas within the class and listening to other children talking about their own development in different areas are ways in which children's understanding can be broadened. As individual children consider their own progress, it is helpful for them to review recorded evidence, and in particular to reconsider notes of their own comments made in previous months or terms. Teacher/child reviews or conferences provide opportunities for teachers to support children in using this evidence. If teachers also share their own records and assessments with children in these discussions, this provides a broader perspective from which children can develop an understanding of their own achievements and needs, and what they must do to move forward in their learning. As this process becomes well established, it helps to ensure that assessment is truly formative, feeding into the forward planning for individual children.

As children become more self-aware, they can be encouraged to review their own work and support reflection by their peers. Opportunities to question others, to read and comment on the work of friends, all support good self-assessment. Children also need time to *think*. Some teachers build in a few minutes at the end of a session specifically for children to reconsider what they have done. Sometimes a longer period of time is set aside when children can consider aspects of their work in some depth and make more detailed written assessments. All these notes can contribute to the teacher's records.

Nevertheless, no matter how effectively children and other adults are involved in the recording process, the class teacher will need to observe children closely and make a range of personal recordings. Even when all sources of help are used effectively, teachers will still need to manage the classroom in ways which free them to observe or work with individuals and groups of children without being constantly interrupted. This is not a new problem, but one which some teachers have attempted to resolve in the past by offering those children, with whom they were not working, very simple, low-level activities, such as colouring in, which were designed to do no more than occupy children's time. In many cases this was not effective in engaging children's interest and effort for any useful length of time. The present demands for wide curriculum coverage militate against such time-wasting but a more fundamental approach is called for, based on good class practice. (One useful approach is described in the following section, pp. 70–71.)

If children are to work independently they need to be encouraged to gradually take control of their learning and to draw on networks of support set up in the classroom which include, but are not exclusively dependent upon, the teacher. If children are to work in autonomous ways they will need to have the confidence to try something new for themselves, to recognise mistakes as part of the learning process and to accept and learn from them rather than fear and conceal them. This can only happen in a classroom where independence is positively encouraged and where children feel secure enough to take risks.

Such independence is often strong in the nursery class, but children can easily come to feel de-skilled on entering infant classes if there are subtle messages that their own knowledge is not valued. Older children too, as they become more aware of the talents of their peers, can become self-conscious and less satisfied with their own performance.

The most important and effective way to build children's confidence and independence is by encouraging them to share their experiences and achievements with their peers. Such recognition values children's work and makes it worthwhile, and is the most important stimulus to independent effort and sustained involvement in activities. Many classes have regular times, often at the beginning and end of the morning, and at the end of the day, for coming together as a class to share experiences, achievements and ideas. While these are valuable, they tend to present sharing times as individual 'bolted on' events. If sharing is to make its fullest contribution to children's development it needs to be part of the wider fabric of class life.

Sharing of finished work is an important feature of most classes, but work and ideas also need to be shared more systematically while they are in progress. When children, individually or as a group, have been set the kind of challenging task which is likely to engage and stimulate them, it is likely to be sustained most effectively if the teacher provides the right opportunities for a group, or the whole class, to pause and share progress. This sharing is a crucial part of independent work: it values what has already been done; allows reflection and the stimulus of new ideas from others in the class, and provides a moment of relaxation, mutual support and appreciation. It is important that such sessions are constructive, and that children leave them feeling refreshed and inspired to take their work forward. The teacher's role in providing support and praise will be important, but much will also depend upon the kind of class ethos already discussed, where children are used to looking positively and constructively at the achievements of their classmates. Children also value the opportunity to share ideas informally, in an on-going way, within pairs and groups, and this kind of exchange can be fostered most successfully in a classroom where talk is encouraged.

Encouragement of independent work will include responsibility for selecting and using materials and information resources. All resources within the classroom must be appropriate to children's needs and be accessible to them –

children should be encouraged to help class management by caring for equipment and by setting it up and clearing it away. For example, specific sets of equipment can be assembled with a checklist, pictorial if necessary, and groups using them should see that they are reassembled clean and complete, and left in the correct place for the next groups's use. When children need pencils, glue, rubbers, etc. they should know where to get them, that they are expected to do so and replace them correctly after use. Labels and notices around the classroom provide both guidance and reading opportunities for children.

Recording reading

Reading is an area where children and other adults, including parents, have been very successfully involved in record-keeping at the basic level of noting what has been read. Children's book reviews have assumed a new significance as evidence for National Curriculum recording of their responses to texts, and even young children's re-writing of favourite stories can reveal their interest in and understanding of story. The teacher will also be making informal records and, from time to time, will wish to spend a longer reading session with the child in order perhaps to make a more careful analysis of their reading strategies through miscue analysis or by using a running record. This can be organised most effectively if children are given the necessary time to prepare a text, and on occasion it may be possible to include an assessment of both a child's ability to respond to a text and their understanding of cross-curricular content.

Occasionally, when the teacher is reading to children, it will be necessary to have a notebook readily to hand in order to take notes on the discussion which follows so that the children's individual responses to a story can be recorded. This kind of observation now forms an important part of the assessment of both reading and talk; assessments will be more reliable, as well as more easily managed, as part of on-going classroom observation at story times.

Recording writing

Primary records of achievement call for children to collect and store their own writing across the curriculum, and this can provide practical assistance for the teacher in compiling evidence. Each child should have a suitable named folder for which they are responsible and to which they have access at all

times. Teachers are using a variety of suitable containers – small lateral filing systems, concertina files, large cardboard boxes and wheeled plastic tubs have all been utilised. As the work is collected some note of context should be provided by the child, the teacher or another adult. Sometimes a teacher may wish to select a particular piece of work as a sample, completing detailed contextual notes on the way the child went about the work, and its significance in terms of writing development. This takes time, but unlike the recording of reading and talk, writing can be assessed out of the classroom when there is an opportunity for the teacher to reflect upon it and give it more detailed consideration.

Increasingly, children are becoming involved in the choice and description of some samples of work through the process of review. Teacher and child together look through the child's folder of work samples, talk about the developments they show and choose pieces as examples of progress. These work samples are then transferred to the school's cumulative records on the child. Children are also encouraged to think about what they want to achieve and set suitable agreed targets with the teacher.

However, such writing reviews make further demands upon classroom time. Some teachers integrate them with planning by holding one or two short reviews at a set time each day, so that even in a large class individual children have this opportunity to talk about their own work with the teacher each half-term. Other teachers feel that such short sessions are not worthwhile, and prefer to spend longer with a child, perhaps only once each term. Such reviews are timetabled in and look more broadly at reading and written work across the curriculum.

Recording talk

The management of observing children and the recording of talk will depend largely on the teacher's success in developing the kinds of independence already described (see pp. 63–65), and the provision of a range of activities which make appropriate demands upon children to plan, investigate, discuss, evaluate and reflect together. Some observation by the teacher can be planned, but revealing comments by children often occur unexpectedly and many teachers have notebooks constantly to hand.

Tape recorders, used selectively, can also help in keeping records of talk. One teacher, concerned by a child's reluctance to

communicate, encouraged him to take a tape recorder into the classroom stock cupboard and make a personal review of his work! In the privacy of his own 'room' the child had the confidence to make detailed and pertinent comments, which he was then happy to share with the teacher. Nevertheless, there are problems with tape recordings: the quality is sometimes poor; individual children's voices are difficult to distinguish and, most important, 'body language', facial expression and some contextual cues are lost. But they can be used effectively in certain situations, for example:

- by acting as a back-up to written observations
- to record one-to-one interviews
- to record pairs of children or small-group discussion which is being observed only occasionally by the teacher, so giving some indication of the way in which the teacher's presence or absence affects the talk
- by being used to record the teacher rather than the children, and allowing teachers to consider their style of presentation and interaction in different situations.

Such recording has the obvious advantage that it can be reviewed in 'non-contact' time, but it needs to be used selectively. It is not worth recording for long periods; there is simply not the time to listen to hours of tape, even if it is of good quality.

Conditions for the development of good record-keeping

Teachers are presented with a typical 'Catch 22' situation in the development of a good system of recording. Good records cannot be established unless there is good classroom practice and effective curriculum management, but good classroom practice and effective curriculum management are themselves a necessary condition for good record-keeping. Perhaps this is why it often proves difficult to break into the circle and establish worthwhile systems. Nevertheless, once in place and operating effectively, a comprehensive recording system provides essential links between planning for individual children, curriculum coverage and development, evaluation and communication, and it will itself make a significant contribution towards efficient management of the classroom. The adoption of the kinds of recording systems

discussed in the previous section clearly represents quite major curriculum development for schools. The benefits are wide ranging, but their very scope indicates the fundamental changes in school and class organisation which they imply. The problems of bringing about change in institutions such as schools have been widely documented, and as M. Fullan points out, change is a process, not an event, which needs careful planning (*The Meaning of Educational Change*).

In a study of the introduction of the Primary Language Record within the Inner London Education Authority in 1989, G. Johnson observed the way schools went about implementing new systems of formative assessment and record-keeping. All ILEA primary schools had been invited to review their language policy and to consider the adoption of the new Record. The programme was an ambitious, innovative one, and the Authority had recognised that it would call for teachers to develop new skills in a whole range of areas. Accordingly, substantial funding had been provided for the organisation of a comprehensive programme of INSET for language co-ordinators and school support through advisory teachers. The clear lead given by the Authority through its commitment to a high quality of recording and the support for schools wishing to develop good practice was fundamental to the success of the programme. However, the initiative was to prove a challenge for individual schools, and a number of factors were identified within the schools themselves which determined their effectiveness in managing the changes in their work necessary for the successful implementation of the Primary Language Record. These factors have relevance for the development of school policy and practice whatever recording system is chosen.

Successful schools had begun by involving the whole staff in a discussion of the school's needs and the decision to adopt the Record. The proposal had been considered in the context of the school development plan, in order to ensure that there was a good basis on which to build, and that a realistic amount of staff time could be given to the work and adequate forward planning done. Short term, achievable goals had been established, and decisions made as to who should be involved and how much of the very detailed record-keeping should be taken on at the outset. Sustained support for staff developing their practice was vitally important, and this was taken forward most successfully where schools had a strong lead from a language co-ordinator with skills in planning school-based INSET – one such co-ordinator organised a comprehensive school-based programme for staff with speakers from within the advisory staff and from other schools.

The role of the head was the most significant factor in the successful introduction of the Primary Language Record. Ideally, heads consulted their staff before volunteering the school for the programme. They instituted the necessary detailed planning and were careful not to overload the staff with too many curriculum initiatives. They were personally committed to the Record and maintained their involvement throughout its introduction, backing the INSET provided by the language co-ordinator, keeping up to date with progress, reading the developing reports and ensuring that time was set aside for staff discussions with parents, with children, and with each other. Without the support of this careful planning, schools were in danger of being overwhelmed by the volume of work, a lack of expertise, or a breakdown in the goodwill and teamwork necessary to sustain the stimulating but demanding programme.

The experiences of these schools demonstrated that the development of recording systems to support the processes of formative assessment involves a complex programme of change, and the skilled management of that change was a factor in their success. Formative assessment touches upon all aspects of children's learning, and challenges teachers to develop their methods of working, class organisation, time management and use of resources. Schools can, nevertheless, meet this challange successfully, and the experiences of one infant school showed how effective teachers can be when they work as a group to take practice forward.

The head and staff of Invicta Infants School in Greenwich had been working for some time to develop aspects of language work within the school and together they considered the new Primary Language Record and decided to adopt it. They met together regularly to review progress and discuss problems, and it soon became apparent that the most difficult aspect of their work was observation of children. There were two problems which had to be resolved in order for them to move forward. One was setting aside time for observation in a busy teaching day, and the other was organising worthwhile activities with which the children could engage independently for any length of time so that the teacher would be free to observe. The language co-ordinator, Val Williamson, commented:

We believed it was important to stand back and observe children, and we needed to encourage them to be autonomous. But we wanted to find activities which were worthwhile and fitted in with good practice and were not just filling time.

The agenda shown here is one from a series of staff meetings at which teachers set out clear aims, for developing practice:

Staff Meeting Invicta School   15 June 1988

Purpose of the meeting is to respond to the concern of staff that the Primary Language Record may take up more time, and there are already not enough hours in the day.

Aims

- to provide an opportunity to reflect upon the meaningful activities already provided in the classrooms and analyse what are the successful elements in them, that seem to engage the children for long periods of time, extend their creativeness and challenge their thinking
- to discuss the elements of structured play
- to share individual expertise, and develop the ideas so as to benefit all children at the school.

NB   If we are successful we should find that we, as teachers, benefit from having longer periods of uninterrupted teaching/observation time enabling us to engage in higher order dialogue with the children, and be more able to put the school's philosophy into practice.

They considered activities which had at one time or another been more than usually successful in supporting sustained concentration and co-operative involvement between children. They identified a number of these and explored the common features which marked them out:

- Why did some role-play areas absorb children's interest and lead to sustained imaginative play?

    The most successful had been those with which children could identify readily, which were rooted in first-hand experiences of some kind and which children had helped to set up. For example, after a visit to a local optician children had furnished the role-play area with display units, eye-testing charts and a reception area and had become absorbed in dramatic play as customers, opticians and receptionists.

- Why were some drawing and modelling activities particularly satisfying for children, supporting concentration and leading to fine, detailed work?

It was found that where children had had an opportunity to examine, handle and discuss real objects and to make drawings and models based on close observations, and where they had been encouraged faithfully to reproduce colours by careful mixing, they had become absorbed in the activity and produced beautifully detailed pictures and models.

- What were the special features of mathematical games which attracted children and kept them involved?

Where children had had a part in devising the games for themselves they had developed a sense of ownership and control and their interest and concentration were sustained for longer periods.

For the most part, these discussions did not lead to the creation of entirely new activities but to the refinement of existing work and, in the course of this, to the affirmation of the school's whole educational philosophy. The practical result was a number of carefully planned learning activities which reflected good practice and fostered independence and collaborative work.

The next step involved facing the practical difficulties of the classroom, and again, a whole-school policy was considered essential. It was decided to set aside an hour on some mornings for all teachers to observe children or to work with a small group. The classes were organised around the planned activities, and no visitors or interruptions were allowed. For the first session the head herself supported the teachers by offering to organise a special activity for up to five children from each class who found it particularly difficult to work independently. The head teacher, Pat Fisher, explained the necessity for this step:

We recognised the importance of detailed observation, especially if it was going to inform future curriculum planning. However, we knew that there were some children who demanded frequent, almost possessive, teacher attention. After discussion I offered to work with some of these children – up to five per class – during that hour period. Interestingly enough, the more the planned activities demanded autonomous behaviour, the fewer the number of children who were identified by staff as needing this kind of support. I recall having only two children from the whole school to work with on one occasion.

The whole approach impacted noticeably on the curriculum offered and on children's learning. I was proud of the high expectations of the staff.

The practical help given to teachers in this way was a temporary measure, designed to support their move into observation. In the event, teachers did not need this help. But the head teacher's offer to work with children was highly significant. It recognised teachers' concerns and helped to resolve them so that the initiative did not present insurmountable problems and founder at the outset. More than this, however, the personal involvement of the head teacher in working alongside staff underlined the importance of observation and recording and the priority it was to be given in the school. The language co-ordinator commented that what had seemed like a daunting task became manageable.

Further such sessions were organised, but as the year progressed teachers found that their skills developed to a point where they were able to observe quite comfortably in the course of normal class work and special 'observation' mornings were phased out. However, at the beginning of the next year, with different groups of children, staff found it necessary to reinstate them.

The success of this school's approach in making significant changes in the way teachers kept records was founded on a number of factors. Staff had a firm basis for the development of good record-keeping through their previous language work. They recognised that the review of observation and recording must be the subject of a whole-school policy which put important issues of class practice under review; development of records was not seen merely as an exercise in designing forms. Staff discussion which gave observation and recording a high priority was accompanied by a frank recognition of difficulties and, in addition, a willingness to confront these and actively seek solutions. Teamwork, the pooling of expertise and the regular review of progress with record-keeping were all a part of the process of development. The involvement of the head and the support of the language co-ordinator underpinned the success of the programme which made an initially daunting task manageable and ultimately led to recording and class practice of a very high order.

Conclusion

The decade of change brought about by the National Curriculum has made it imperative for schools to develop systems for coping with the increasing demands of assessment, and the effects of this work have been wide ranging. The issues of classroom management raised by the pace and scope of these developments have brought staff together to evaluate practice and work out whole-school approaches, particularly in the area of record-keeping. These shared records have supported greater team work and the development of a common language and philosophy as staff in primary schools decide together what should count as progress and development.

A further outcome of the work on record-keeping has been teachers' own professional development. Teachers who engage in a high quality of recording report that they are teaching more effectively: they are more informed about language and literacy and better able to respond to the needs of individual children. Their record-keeping also acts as a check on subjectivism; where teachers are able to look at children in a more structured way and give them more equal attention, their assessments are likely to prove more accurate.

The impetus that has been given to teachers' records by the introduction of the National Curriculum has been a positive and important development. What such records could perhaps ultimately offer is a means of evaluating the content of the National Curriculum itself. This curriculum, especially in the younger age groups, is not based on any detailed evidence of what children in the Key Stages can actually do. But plenty of such evidence is currently available in the form of teachers' records, which now constitute perhaps the most detailed body of evidence that exists of children's learning in the primary school. The National Curriculum Council should be drawing on this valuable evidence when reviewing the content of the Programmes of Study and their associated Attainment Targets, and when drawing out the lessons to be learnt from the first few years of the implementation of the new curriculum.